Startup

Use Connections to Build Your Silicon Valley Seed Startup

Second Edition 2019

Andreas Ramos

andreas.com

Copyright

Startup (second edition) by Andreas Ramos. All rights reserved. © 2019 Andreas Ramos USA. ISBN: 9781729381335. Independently published

This document is protected by copyright. No part of this document may be reproduced in any form by any means without prior written permission from the author.

Second Edition, January 2019

For the second edition, I updated, deleted, and added sections, including chapter ten on acquisitions. The book has also been translated to Spanish, French, and Korean. You can get this book on paper, digital (Kindle), and audio podcast. For more information, see the book's webpage.

After January 1st, 2020, see the book's webpage for updates.

The Website for this Book

Go to andreas.com/book-startup.html

All links in the book are clickable links at the book's webpage at andreas.com/book-startup.html

Did You Find an Error?

If you see errors, let me know so I can fix them. Please include the page number or sentence so I can find it.

Have a Comment or Idea?

Let me know! Send me an email (andreas@andreas.com). I'll make changes for the update.

Layout and Production

Cover by Ginger Namgostar. Layout by Anaximander Katzenjammer. Soundtrack by Eliza Rickman, Coeur de Pirate, and Zaz on Pandora.

Dedication

For Gong Zhihong and Anaximander Katzenjammer

About the Author

I've started three startups. I'm an advisor to fifteen startups. I've worked at more than thirty Silicon Valley startups. I worked at SGI and SUN and was head of the digital agency at Acxiom and the Manager of Global SEO at Cisco. I teach at INSEEC SF, a French business school in San Francisco, written twelve books on SEO, graduated from Universität Heidelberg, and have a house in Palo Alto with my wife and cat.

- For more about me, visit andreas.com
- You're welcome to write to me at andreas@andreas.com
- Sign up for my newsletter at eepurl.com/wC-C1 or my website

Translations

This book was translated into Spanish by Edgar Estanislao (California) and edited by Gala Gil Amat (Spain). It was translated into Korean by Dale Ho Kim in South Korea and French by Cyril Ghattas in France.

Trademarks

Names of companies and products are trademarks, registered trademarks, or trade names of their respective holders, and have been used in an editorial fashion only. Infringement, endorsement, or affiliation isn't intended. Blah, blah, blah.

Promotional Consideration

I mention companies, software, books, and so on because they're useful for you. I don't get paid by them.

Table of Contents

Let's Get Started 5
1: You and Your Seed Startup 8
2: Your Founder Team 22
3: Building the Company 34
4: Interview Your Customers 53
5: Develop Your Product 67
6: Legal Stuff 74
7: Funding Stuff 87
8: Boring Stuff: Finances 117
9: Selling Your Startup 120
10: The Acquisition 134
    The Players on Your Side 138
    Position Your Startup for Acquisition 148
    The Negotiation 150
    The Big Picture 158
    Conclusion 160
    Further Reading 160
11: Life after Your Startup 162
In Closing 164
Extra Stuff 165
Index 166

Let's Get Started

Who Is this Book For?

You have an idea and you want to build a startup. You start by building a seed startup.

What this Book Is

I've written this book to give you an overview of how to build a Silicon Valley (SV) early-stage startup. This book covers:

- How to build your team of co-founders and advisors
- Develop your idea
- Build digital presence
- When to incorporate
- Dealing with stocks
- Dealing with funding
- How to sell your startup

Who Is this Book Not For?

If you want a quiet 9-5 job, join an established company.

The Interviews

I interviewed 26 founders of startups, heads of accelerators, and VCs to learn about the reality of doing startups in Silicon Valley, Denmark, Finland, Sweden, France, Germany, Spain, China, India, South Korea, Colombia, Indonesia, plus Hawaii, Florida, and New York.

Often, after I talk about something, I add the founders' experience. Sometimes they contradict each other and that's okay. There are many paths to the top.

There's a full list of founders and their website at the book's webpage.

➔ When I add a founder's comments, I'll mark it with an arrow.

Founders include: Brienne Ghafourifar (SV), Oscar Gomez (Colombia), Gala Gil Amat (Spain), Sandro Groganz (Germany), Dick Brunebjerg (Denmark), Joseph Biley (Cote d'Ivoire, West Africa), Jules Peysson (France), Scott Stouffer (SV), Lars Birkemose (Denmark), Kenneth Low (Singapore), Nick Hurd (Hawaii), Camille Belin (France), Sarah Green Brodersen (Denmark), Virginie Glanzer (NYC), Clement Gonthier (France), Maruf Yusupov (Denmark), Mehdi Coly (France), Andrea Lynn Cianflone (NYC), Wei Nie (China), Yeni Kim (South Korea), Varun & Rahul Aggarwal (India), and Chris Beach (US).

Many people gave me great ideas. Thanks to (alphabetically): Adrian Rodriguez, Alston Ghafourifar, Barry Simon, Bob Chunn, Mehdi Ghafourifar, Ronda Broughton, Vera Kryukova, Zhihong Gong, and the students at INSEEC SF.

I also thank David Smith's *Zero to IPO*, Mahendra Ramsinghani's *The Business of Venture Capital*, and Y-Combinator's lectures.

I talked with heads of accelerators: Claire Chang of IgniteXL in Redwood City; Steve Hoffman of Founders Space in San Francisco; plus angels and VCs.

For chapter ten, *The Acquisition*, I interviewed (alphabetically): Alain Labat, investment banker at Harvest Management Partners; David Smith, attorney, 100 acquisitions; Donna Petkanic, attorney at Wilson Sonsini Goodrich & Rossati, 20 acquisitions; Eric Milliken, attorney at Sutter Legal, +200 startups; George Kopas, Advisor, UC Berkeley; Patrick Chung, attorney and VC; Shawn Flynn, Sr. Bizdev at Tech Code, and several more people. The chapter was reviewed by Ed Ipser, IpserLabs.com; George Parrish, Entrepreneur's Lab; Ron Morris, INSEEC; and Tim Koltek, Koltek.com.

A Few Notes about the Text

- Instead of writing "products and services" each time, I'll just write "products."
- Some people may wonder why I explain words and ideas "that everyone knows." This book will be read in China, Africa, and Asia where common American words such as pitching mean nothing. Even Americans don't know some of these ideas. I've found many people have never seen a milestone. Hint: it's not something in an office.
- I wrote this book so everyone can read it. If you don't understand a word or sentence, let me know and I'll rewrite it.
- When I write $10, that's ten US dollars. When I write $10M or $10B, that's ten million or ten billion.
- Some people ask, why don't I write in a formal business style? Oh, just be glad I used punctuation. Actually, there's a reason for this. Startups are intensely personal. You get to know your co-founders really well. There's no point in being formal.
- There is a list of clickable links at andreas.com/book-startup.html. You can also type the URL (such as t2m.io/ygUYWg8E).
- Why is this book so short? Other startup books are 400 pages. People like short books.

Any more questions? No? Good. Let's start.

1: You and Your Seed Startup

What Is a Seed Startup?

There are several stages in Silicon Valley startups.

- Seed Stage: A few people have an idea, build a team, and interview users and build a product to see if there is a viable business model. They get a few advisors. They may join incubators and accelerators. If the idea looks good, they get funding from family, friends, and angels. Seed startups are also called early-stage startups.

- Mid-stage Startup: The project turns into a business, which means it get customers and starts to make money. Hire a few staffers and contractors. Set up early marketing, sales, and metrics. Get more funding from angels and perhaps VCs.

- Late-Stage Startup: The project turns into an ongoing business that makes money. Hire directors and staff. Investment in marketing and sales for growth. Add departments. Funding from angels and VCs. Also known as the growth stage.

After that, you sell the company, merge into another company, do an IPO, or run the company forever.

There aren't clear definitions for the stages of startups. Founders and investors also have different goals, so they use different names and definitions. And it's all evolving anyway.

In this book, we'll cover only seed startups: how to develop your idea and get started.

People use both "seed" and "early-stage" to describe new startups so I'll switch back and forth between both terms in this book.

So What's a Startup?

For a while, a startup meant a technical company in Silicon Valley.

But now, practically all companies use technology. Is Uber a technology company or a taxi company that uses software? Every year, the definition is less clear. I'll focus on technology startups, but this book can be used for many other kinds of businesses.

What's a Connected Startup?

Key Idea: A startup is successful if it has strong connections among founders, advisors, investors, and customers.

For outsiders, Silicon Valley is technology and digital tools. But Silicon Valley is actually a complex web of personal connections who share resources and information: where to find co-founders, advisors, investors, and customers. How to build startups for very little money. The best technical solutions. What works or doesn't work. People and tools to avoid. It's connections.

That's what I learned by writing this book and talking with dozens of founders, advisors, and investors. That's the most important idea in this book. If you learn only one thing, learn how to build and grow your connections.

Whatever field you work in, it's connections. In every field that I've worked with, I've found a deep network of experts who've been working in that field for 15 or 20 years, know the field extremely well, and they all know each other. If you want to succeed, you have to become part of the network.

What Is Silicon Valley?

From the 1930s to the 1990s, Silicon Valley (SV) was based on engineering that built things: chips, hard disks, routers, and so on.

In the mid-90s, Silicon Valley evolved into the Internet and the web. Yahoo! and Google were built. Social media started in the mid-2000s with Facebook, Instagram, Pinterest, and others. Silicon Valley is now web-based companies, so it should be called *Digital Valley*.

Three things work together in Silicon Valley:

- Startups, which are teams of founders and advisors who create companies. There are around 30,000 startups in Silicon Valley (see t2m.io/7nhqpzG5).
- Money, which is invested in startups by angels who made money in their startups or venture capitalists (VCs) who manage investor money.
- Legal services, which includes incorporation, contracts, intellectual property (IP), patents, copyrights, and trademarks, which are handled by lawyers, along with services by mergers and acquisitions (M&A) and investment bankers (IBs) who prepare startups for sale or initial public offering (IPO).

These three things (ideas, money, and legal stuff) are tied together by connections.

Where Is Silicon Valley?

Like everything else about Silicon Valley, its location is also changing.

When I came to Silicon Valley in the early 90s, it was Palo Alto and a few small cities around it: Mountain View, Sunnyvale, Santa Clara, and Cupertino. It really was a small valley between two low mountain ranges.

In the late 90s, SV expanded into the triangle between the 101, 237, and 880 freeways. What used to be vast orchards of fruit trees became Cisco and many web-based companies.

By the mid-2000s, SV stretched from San Mateo to north San Jose and across to Fremont.

In the early 2010s, SV added San Francisco's startups as it spread through what we call "the Greater Bay Area," a triangle of about ten million people from Marin county to Tahoe and down to Monterey.

At some point, Silicon Valley globalized. What once was a few small towns in a small valley turned into a global network. It's mostly web-based, so it doesn't matter where teams live. Free video conference calling, email, and file sharing make it possible to work anywhere. When people are working from home, they can be on early morning calls with Europe and late evening calls with China and India. SV is probably the world's most globalized area where 74% of SV's workers are from another country (see t2m.io/3gP668df, p. 14).

Silicon Valley is now worldwide. That's why I interviewed people in China, India, Europe, Africa, South America, and the US.

You can build your Silicon Valley startup anywhere in the world. You can get ideas and experience from Silicon Valley startups, see what works in your country and city, use the web to connect and work with people in SV, and build your startup wherever you are. What happened in the last twenty years in Silicon Valley will happen in the next twenty years all over the world.

Startupping in Three Steps

Here's a quick overview. We'll go through each of these in this book.

- You build a small team of co-founders and advisors.
- Talk with customers to find problems that cost them time or money.
- Based on those interviews, you build products to solve those problems. You should to be able to know within six to eight weeks if your product will work.
- When you can show there are sufficient customers, the product saves them time and money, and they will pay for it, investors will be interested. At that point, you switch from seed stage to a mid-stage startup, where you get investor money, incorporate, get a bank account, and accept funding. You use the investors' money to build marketing and sales which will produce revenues. When you get customers, you'll add support.
- Finally, there is the exit. Either you sell the seed startup or the late-stage startup to a large company and they do more sales and marketing. You collect $10m, share the money with your co-founders and investors, and buy your private beach.

See? Only three steps!

There is also lots of paperwork, such as incorporation, lawyers, contracts, accountants, and so on. This is just stuff you have to do, like getting your teeth cleaned. Do this only just to get it done. Your real job is your team, your customers, and your product.

"Wait, weren't there more than three steps in that list?" Just seeing if you're paying attention.

What It Will Cost

In the mid-90s, you needed about twenty million dollars to build a startup. These were mini-companies, so you needed server admins, IT support, accounting and finance, HR, secretaries, receptionists, janitors, and other people. You had to buy computers, servers, telephone systems, and so on. Advertising was done on nationwide radio, TV, and newspapers, which was expensive.

Today, you can do the early-stage phase for very little money. How small is "very little money"? If your app will be in the Apple App Store, you need an Apple app developer license ($100). You should use Google Ads (formerly known as "Google Adwords") to test keywords (for product names), phrases (for slogans, pitches, tagline), and logos. You can do this for about $100-$200. If you sign up for Google Analytics (and if you don't, don't ever talk to me), you'll get $150 credit from Google. you can do the seed stage for the first three-to-six months for $100 to $200.

What Do I Have to Know about Startups?

You'll be doing two things at the same time: developing your product and building the business side of your startup.

You must understand the legal stuff and the implications of incorporation, which includes how to divide the stock. If you want funding, everyone on the founder team must understand what investors want and how they work. You need to understand how much stock you get, both in the number of shares and the percentage of the company, and how you'll be affected by dilution. You also need to understand how preferred stock will give most of the money to the investors.

What about Incorporation, Lawyers, and Funding?

- To receive $2m from an investor, you need a business bank account to hold the money.
- To get a business bank account, you need an EIN number (Employer Identification Number).
- To get an EIN number, you incorporate.

You do all of this towards the end of your seed startup. First, you form a team and find out if you have a product. When that's done, you start the process for funding. When an investor gives you money, you incorporate, get the business bank account, and deposit the check.

Many startups incorporate at the beginning while they're still developing the product or even before they start developing. This is a mistake. First, it takes time to do this and you shouldn't waste time. Secondly, it costs about $2,000 to incorporate (and if you don't know what you're doing, lawyers may charge $20-30,000). Finally, if you discover the idea won't work, you've lost time and money. Wait until you get an investor and use that money to incorporate.

What You'll Need

You only need a few things:

- Confidence: Trust in yourself that you'll give it a good try. Ignore the whiners and negativists.
- Commitment: You gotta work super hard for a year or two.
- Perseverance. Nearly all of the founders whom I interviewed have something in common: they don't take no. They pushed and pushed to make things happen. You will run into many closed doors; just push harder until they open. And if the door doesn't open, knock out a window and climb in.

You don't need much more than this. Okay, maybe a computer :-)

➔ I noticed nearly all of the founders were really happy. They work 12-14 hour days for six days per week but they're okay with that because they're doing what they really want and nobody tells them what to do. When you're doing that, it's not work. And definitely not boring.

➔ You also need courage. You need courage to quit what you've been doing and start something that you've never done before and don't know if it'll work.

Why Not Just Get a Job?

Shouldn't you just get a job at a large company? Isn't that safer?

Jobs have a downside. Companies want workers who fit in the process. This means you won't learn much. There's no job security because companies fire people to improve their quarterly numbers (and when that happens, VPs get a bonus, so VPs want to fire staffers).

But don't companies pay better in the long run? To keep your job, you have to produce roughly 4X your salary. If they pay you $100,000 per year, then you have to produce $400,000 for the company. Would you make $400,000 and give $300,00 to somebody else? If you think that's a good idea, send your money to me.

How Do I Get a Job at a Seed Startup?

As you'll see in this book, early-stage startups don't hire people. They're a small group of founders, advisors, and investors. If founders get any money, it covers their costs.

People get hired at Facebook and Twitter, but those aren't seed startups.

You also won't get training at a seed startup. You'll get massive responsibility but nobody helps you. One time, an intern joined at 9 a.m. At 10 a.m., I took him to a major client meeting. Before we went in, I told him if he said he was an intern, they'd send him out to get coffee, so I introduced him as a director. We got the project so at 1 pm, I turned it over to him. "What'll I do?" "I gotta go to another meeting. Figure it out."

But you're wondering, don't people get jobs at startups, get a big salary and lots of stock, and when it IPOs, they get rich? Like in the movies?

Yes, it happens… but… 19 out of 20 startups fail. You'll be exhausted, your stock will be worthless, most of your salary will pay for Silicon Valley's expensive housing and food, and you'll never see your dog.

Instead of getting a job, build a startup. Your dog will look up to you.

If you still want to work at a mid-stage or late-stage startup, see angel.co.

➔ If you want to build a startup, but don't have the connections or know what to do, you could join a startup and learn. A year in a startup is like seven years anywhere else.

Silicon Valley's Iceberg

You only see the top of an iceberg. 92% of the iceberg is underwater.

Just like icebergs, you don't see most of Silicon Valley. People go to conferences, hack events, and pitch nights but they don't see the connections, relationships, and experience.

Many meetings happen in Palo Alto backyards, often on at night, often on weekends. Silicon Valley is deep, personal connections between experts.

One thing about SV that amazes visitors (asides from totally blue skies and great food :-) is the openness and cooperation. Nearly everywhere else in the world, business people are secretive and generally unhelpful. For whatever reason, people in SV share ideas, information, and resources.

Grow Your Connections

You don't get connections; you build connections. Talk with people and show them what you're doing. They'll introduce you to more people. They include:

- Advisors who have founded three startups and have ten years of experience.
- The directors of business schools and professors have taught many students who've gone on to set up companies. They also consult for companies and know investors.
- Heads of incubators and accelerators who work with startups and investors.
- Heads of investor groups know other investors.
- Venture capital firms include the general partners, associates, junior associates, analysts, and interns. Many of them are active in Silicon Valley events and they're constantly looking for startups.

If you're in your early 20s, you have about thirty years in your career ahead of you. By building startups, one after the other, you'll build up a great deal of connections. They'll help you in your career.

If you show that you can build a viable business, investors will come to you. When Mark Zuckerberg came to Palo Alto, he didn't have to go to investors. They stood in line to meet him.

➔ One founder said if there is one tip for new founders, it's to get experienced advisors with lots of connections. Keep your advisors involved in your project and reach out to their network. Their startup has 30 advisors which made it possible to raise funding entirely through personal networks and not go to VCs.

➔ Several said it's all about connections. If you're an insider, people will meet with you and talk with you. But if you don't build connections, it's very difficult to get in.

Professor Alex Pentland at MIT tracked millions of trades on eToro, an online trading service for day traders, which also has a social network where traders can share ideas and strategies. He found traders were either isolated or were densely connected to other traders. The highly-connected traders earned 30% more than isolated traders.

Reid Hoffman, founder of LinkedIn, spoke at a Y-Combinator event. He sold LinkedIn to Microsoft for $26B and has been a VC since 2010. Sam Altman asked him how many startup proposals he got every year. Hoffman said about 6,000. And how many do you read? None. Delete them. You don't read any of them? No, I delete them all. But aren't you going to miss a few good ideas? No, because if the person doesn't have the connections to give it to someone who knows me, then he doesn't have the connections to find co-founders. He doesn't have the connections to hire staff. He doesn't have the connections to meet investors. He doesn't have the connections to find customers. If he can't get the proposal to me through connections, he will probably fail.

SV Dress Code

What to wear in Silicon Valley? Just like everywhere, there are standards. Not much, but some.

Everyone looks like a Berkeley graduate student. Polo shirt or T-shirt, jeans, and running shoes. In summer, shorts and sandals.

In New York, they wear ties. Don't wear a tie in Silicon Valley; it says "clueless."

This T-shirts and jeans stuff can be a problem. If you're in New York and a barefooted guy in a long beard, an old T-shirt, and torn jeans talks to you, you yell for the police.

But in Palo Alto, I often saw Steve Jobs at a nearby café and he was in a T-shirt, old jeans, and barefoot. People in SV care about your technical skills and little else.

Your Digital Presence

Okay, T-shirts and jeans. What else do you need?

You need to be findable on the web so people, investors, and customers can find you. This means:

- Personal website: This can be a one-page site. Use Wordpress or whatever.
- Professional photo: Really, get a professional photo. Don't use a snapshot. If you have to, go to the kiddie photographer at the mall and get the $25 special with the bunny ears.
- Page in Crunchbase, Angle.co, LinkedIn, Facebook, WeChat, and Twitter.
- Phone and email: Get a US telephone number and an email address from your startup (or use Gmail).

➜ A founder added: To get a US number, buy a SIM card at T-Mobile on a $3/month plan (and pre-pay for one year). When you're in the US, use the SIM card and go to T-Mobile and pay $40 for one month of phone + Internet data.

On your website and social profiles, show relevant credentials, experience, and expertise. The word is "relevant." For example, you have a degree in computer science from University of Geneva and your team won two hackathons. Don't talk about your certificate in puppy training.

You also need business cards. It's a bit odd, but these are still popular.

You (and co-founders) really need to have a digital presence so when investors and customers research you, you show up. If you don't show up, it doesn't look good.

You should also make sure your social profiles show you in a good light. Investors and advisors, and large customers may look at these pages. Look at what's been posted about you in Facebook, Twitter, and so on and remove what shouldn't be there.

If you have common name and can't be found in Google, use Google Ads. Add your name as a keyword in quotation marks and brackets ("john smith" and [john smith]) and create an ad for yourself. Set the bid at $0.25 with a $1 daily budget.

Your Startup Workweek

If a work week is 40 hours, then a 60-hour week is 150%. One of the interviewed founders has been working 340% for five months.

But don't count the hours. You'll be working efficiently so you'll do more in a week than staffers do in two months.

In SV, we call that dog years. It's an American thing. People say one year in a dog's life is like seven years for people. A two-year old dog is like a 14-year old teenager. You'll do more in one year in your startup than seven years elsewhere.

Tho' many founders work every day for 3-6 months, I recommend that you relax on Sundays. If you get exhausted, you won't work well.

➔ Is it hard work? No, nearly all of the founders agreed that they really enjoy it because they're doing what they really want to do. It's actually harder to work 40 hours per week for a company because that's boring.

Why You Do Startups

As long as you don't take funding, you have the freedom to do what you want. The #1 Rule in Silicon Valley is "There Are No Rules in Silicon Valley!"

➔ One of the founders said she loved the unbounded creativity of building startups. Many others said that doing it for the money or to build companies is the wrong reason. You should do it because you love to create.

➔ Some of the founders told me that they learned about themselves. After a while, they realized they really wanted a stable company of their own. They didn't want a large company with hundreds of staff which becomes a treadmill. Big sounds good but people who do startups generally want to do hands-on development.

Personal Impact

Finally, a few notes about how a startup will affect your life. Endless work is exhausting. Your body will hurt from sitting too much. That nightclub stuff is only in the movies. You'll be at your computer Saturday night at 3 a.m.

Startups are also bad for relationships. A startup is more intense than a relationship. It's a great way to get divorced. Your partner should accept you're going to disappear for a year or two.

Take breaks. Go to the redwoods, Santa Cruz beaches, Big Sur, Pinnacles National Park, Yosemite, the Grand Canyon, Horseshoe Bend, Lower Antelope Canyon, and Zion National Park. Go where there are no bars.

When I say "no bars," I mean no bars on your cell phone reception.

Don't take your laptop. Our team once went to Hawaii; some of the developers stayed in the hotel rooms and wrote code.

You can go to Maui (or Santa Cruz) and lay on the beach where you'll look at the waves and watch the birds until you start thinking about how much money you're losing by laying on the beach.

Remember the upside: you're doing something nobody has done and everyone will use.

➜ First-time founders talked about the lack of experience and uncertainty. Everything is new, everything has to be figured out, and it all has to be done at once. There's lots of frustration over wasted time. It's also scary when you realize that everything can fail and you've wasted a whole year on nothing.

The Long View

Okay, a bit of bad news. If this is your first startup, you'll likely fail. Too much to learn, too much to do all at the same time, too many mistakes, and you'll be exhausted and overwhelmed.

Some of you will end up just trying to survive. There are lots of costs, little money, and everyone doubts what you're doing. You'll even begin to doubt yourself. Mark Zuckerberg didn't think Facebook was worthwhile.

Doing a startup is like solving a very complicated puzzle where you suspect the instructions are for another puzzle, some of the parts are missing, and there's nobody to ask. When you change one thing, other things change in unseen ways.

If it's not working, talk with your advisors and quit early. Don't let a weak idea drag out for a long time. It's good to fail fast because you'll be able to start the next project.

The good news in failure is that you'll learn how to put together and lead a team and how to build relationships with advisors, investors, customers, and vendors. If you fail but you did a good job at it, your team will follow you to your next startup. Nearly all of the interviews agreed that your second and third startup will be better.

Just like falling off a horse, you get up, dust yourself off, and get back on.

And yes, I've fallen off several times from galloping horses.

What's the Future for Startups?

As I wrote earlier, SV has now created a global market for Internet, web, and technology. It's no longer just the US market or the German market. You can sell world-wide.

➜ One of the interviews pointed out that there are many new technologies such as IoT, AI, machine learning, 3D printing, biotech, blockchain, and so. These will create new platforms, which will have dozens of new companies around it, plus hundreds more to service those companies. For example, the concept of social media created an eco-system of social media companies, hundreds of tools, and thousands of agencies. There will be thousands of new startups. What we have today is only 1% of what there will be.

Is that really possible? When I got on the web, there were only a few thousand people (which is why I have andreas.com). We had no idea it would grow to two billion people. The web will double in the next ten years.

More about Palo Alto

There's more about Palo Alto: where to go, eat, buy stuff, and so on. See andreas.com/what-to-see-in-silicon-valley.html

Summary: A Founder's Story

➜ A founder from Spain came to Palo Alto for Stanford University's summer entrepreneur course. She met her professors and students. She also got to know the head of her dorm, who graduated in computer science. He introduces her to the other Stanford students, including mechanical engineers and computer science students. One Chinese student is a mechanical engineer at Brown. A friend in London was doing a startup a few years ago and I'm an advisor. He tells her to talk with me.

I introduce her to another founder in Germany, whom I had met at a conference in Denmark. The German founder introduces her to his lawyer in SF. I introduce her to a former VC who becomes her funding advisor. Nearly every day after class, she goes to events and conferences and meets more people. We all go out for Sichuan Chinese food and a Thai student comes along who is studying medicine at Stanford. Her boyfriend is a mechanical engineer at UC Berkeley. He wants to learn about startups so he comes down to Palo Alto to talk with me and he gets involved with her project. She has to deliver a business plan, which we write in two hours. Her Stanford professor introduces her to multinational company which is interested in buying her company. After the Stanford classes are over, she stays ten days in our house and continues to meet people in Silicon Valley. She works with the SF lawyer and begins incorporation. In early September, her valuation is $1m. By late October, it's $4m. She returns to Spain. In December, she comes back to Palo Alto to pitch in San Francisco and stays at our house for another two weeks to meet with more Stanford professors, CEOs, VCs, investors, lawyers, founders, and students. She returned in March to pitch at a conference for global insurance companies and present her prototype.

Is she special? No. I'm working with another startup that was started by an 18-year old girl. She has raised $15m and has a $150m valuation.

2: Your Founder Team

Okay, the last chapter was the fun stuff (wait, 120 hours a week in a chair is the fun stuff?)

Let's talk about the most important part of your startup: your founder team. This is the hard core of two to four people that builds the seed startup.

Your co-founders should be involved in everything: strategy, technology, operations, funding, finance, legal, and so on. Some of you can focus in areas, but everyone should help to manage the startup. Hold group discussion and make decisions by consensus.

You as the Key Founder

You build the team. You find people for your team, you interview them, you accept or reject people.

You also keep them motivated. You'll deal with pushback and negativity.

Your job is to inspire and lead. Decide if issues are important or unimportant. Delegate as much as possible. In general, prevent riots and put out fires.

Ask your team for suggestions, feedback, and advice, but be the leader. You lead and they will follow. This means you make decisions, both good decisions and unpopular decisions.

➜ Founders said you should evangelize your company. That means you promote your startup by speaking at fundraising, going to pitch events, and talking with everyone.

➜ Several founders told me they have to lead the meetings, otherwise, the co-founders and others just wait. Encourage them to start without you. That's the difference between Real Madrid, the world's #1 soccer team, and a local soccer team: at Real Madrid, the players start practice even if the coach doesn't show up.

➜ Founders are involved in every aspect of the company: strategy, team leadership, marketing, sales, relations with other companies, contracts, and so on. And many of them are still in college so they're also in classes and taking exams.

Problems with Leaders

Team problems are usually leader problems.

If the leader often shows up late, goes on frequent vacations, or is a jerk, the others will start showing up late, taking off, playing computer games, or be difficult. If he starts missing regular meetings, people see it's not important. If there's too much arguing, the leader isn't leading or he brought in people who like to be difficult.

Some startups have problems with sexism. The guys start acting like jerk brogrammers and harass the women developers. The leader has to stop it. If he doesn't, it gets out of control and people leave.

➜ There are several kinds of CEO problems. A stubborn CEO may listen to advisors and experts, but he'll go back to his original idea and refuse to change. Another kind of difficult CEO is the ones who won't focus. They jump from idea to idea and won't finish one. Some CEOs insist on perfection and won't allow a product to be released to the market because it can always be better.

The leader should lead by example: be the first to arrive and the last to leave. If everyone works remotely, the leader should stay in touch with everyone and be the first on conference calls. The leader should be at all meetings.

Co-Founders

You should have two or three co-founders.

You shouldn't do a startup alone because there are too many things to do.

At least one of your co-founders should have technical skills. If your team doesn't have someone with relevant technical skills, your team won't really understand your industry. It will be very expensive to pay for technical development. An MBA isn't a technical skill. MBAs are taught to manage companies, not start them. Of the 50 largest companies at Forbes, only five CEOs are MBAs. The rest are techies.

Other founders, investors, and customers will look at your team. If you have a good team, they'll join. Choose co-founders based on credentials, experience, and expertise. Don't add someone because you were friends in college.

Spend several months with someone before you ask him to be a co-founder. Ask him to do some work for free. See if he does it for the passion. If he wants money, you don't want him as a co-founder.

If she's a graduate student, is working on a grant, or is working at a company, you need to look at her contracts and agreements. Many universities and nearly all companies write in their contracts that they own all rights to any intellectual property that the person created. You'll have to get a release from the university or company.

This also means if one of your co-founders has a day job, she can't use her office computer at work or the company laptop at home. She can't work on your startup during work hours. If the company pays for her cell phone, she can't use that either. Any work done on a company device is owned by the company.

➔ One of the founders told me that he has no co-founders. However, it's his fifth startup and he has a good executive team and six advisors, so his investors didn't mind that he is a solo founder. If this is your first startup, investors may want to see co-founders who can share the work.

➔ Another way to learn about potential co-founders is to do a few small projects together. Build a website for someone or write code. You'll see how they do things, collaborate, and share information.

How to Find Co-founders

You could look at angel.co for people who want to join companies. But that's a bit random.

The best way to find co-founders is through your personal network. Talk with everyone: your advisors, professors, classmates, and so on.

Problems with Co-founders

Co-founders are like cats. They're very smart and do only what they want and only when they feel like it.

Be sure a co-founder is fully committed before you bring her aboard. If she starts and then quits a few months later, it will demoralize the team.

You've also wasted time. Investors will also ask questions why she left.

You should also be careful if a co-founder brings many of her friends to the team. They're on her side and if she leaves, they may leave with her.

There should also be a plan for dealing with co-founder problems. At the beginning, everyone is friends, but sometimes, serious differences will come up. Sometimes, people refuse to agree. You should have a plan for arbitration by a neutral third person whom everyone accepts, such as a senior advisor or professor.

➔ One of the main reasons for startup failure is the inability to agree. A founder told me that she started her first company with a co-founder and they immediately split the company 50/50 without a vesting plan. The company quickly began to make money. The co-founder also realized that she got half of the money, so after three months, she stopped working. The founder was unable to get her to work. After nine months, the founder quit the company. I've heard of this at several more companies.

➔ A co-founder has to be involved 150%. That's a 60-hour week. Some join but after a while, they sit back and let you lead. They may see themselves as a staff employee who do what they're told and nothing more. Some founders said in their first startup, co-founders simply stopped working after a few months. In several cases, the co-founders had no relevant skills and were pushed in because they were relatives of investors. It was impossible to get rid of them. One co-founder did nothing for nine months. When the startup took off, the team didn't want to give her any part of it. She sued to get money and the team had to pay to get rid of the lawsuit.

➔ In the eagerness to get started, people rush into setting up teams, so they often pick wrong people. For example, they start companies with their best friends. When the company falls apart, they won't talk with each other again.

➔ Often, people can't communicate with their partners about the stress, lack of money, lack of time, or missing resources. A co-founder has to learn to say what he needs to say to the other co-founders and be able to listen to the other co-founders. It helps to set clear priorities and goals along with clear lines for areas of responsibility and decision-making. The team has to accept that one co-founder is the leader and they will accept the leader's final decisions.

→ The agreement between co-founders should include a section for outside arbitration and terms for separation.

Serial Founder or Serial Entrepreneur?

Some people say they want to be serial founders. That's like a little kid saying that when he grows up, he wants to be married five times. Perhaps he will study at Trump University?

Again, don't add anyone who is looking for money.

→ This includes marketing and sales people. I've met founders who had talked with marketing people who offered to do the marketing for 40%. That's a ridiculous request; if someone asks for that, he doesn't know what he's doing.

Advisors

You should also have advisors.

Look for advisors who have built at least three startups as founders. They should also have ten years of experience in your field and be ten years ahead of you.

Ask them about their experience, how they failed, and what they learned.

They can save you a great deal of time and money by showing you how to do it smaller, cheaper, faster.

Every major decision should be reviewed by your advisors. Listen to their advice and make your own decision.

Advisors should neutral. They shouldn't have a conflict of interest. They shouldn't get referral fees for steering you to a vendor.

Advisors can introduce you to their network to get co-founders, contractors, side jobs, lawyers, funding, leads, and customers.

Be careful with corporate people as advisors. They'll advise you to do things the corporate way. That's nice for corporations, but not startups.

Some American schools have a problem where the big kids beat up the little kids and steal their lunch money. To solve this, many schools started a big brother / big sister project, where little kids are matched up with big kids. The big kids protect them from bad kids on the playground and make sure they get into the good teams.

In a way, advisors are big brothers or big sisters for your startup. There are bad boy VCs, investors, lawyers, or recruiters who will mislead you and overcharge you in money or stock. Advisors will warn about you them. Advisors may also introduce you to good lawyers and investors who will work with you and charge fair fees.

You can have several kinds of advisors:

- Senior advisor: A senior advisor is deeply involved in overall strategy and is also an expert on various topics. He advises you on salaries, investments, stock distribution, and so on. He helps to bring in additional people. He may be hands-on, almost like a co-founder.
- Skills advisor: They're experts in areas such as operations, legal, finance, funding, SEO, digital marketing, social marketing, sales, and so on. You may end up with five or six skills advisors.
- Names: These are high-profile persons that you add as advisors because it looks good, but you rarely talk with them. For example, you can have Bill Gates or Mark Zuckerberg as an advisor.

You give stock to advisors, depending on how much they do for you. The amount is up to you. We'll discuss this later in the chapter on legal stuff.

➔ The amount of stock also depends on the stage of the company. In the first three to six months, there can be a lot of intense work so they should get more. After a year or so, new advisors will join an established operation where they'll spend less time, so you can give less.

➔ Your advisors should look out for you, like your big brother or big sister. You should have frequent lunches or dinners with them and be able to talk openly about a problem from all sides.

➔ Some of the founders are the fourth generation of families that do business. This gave them access to an extensive network of people with business expertise who shared freely. Look through your extended family of uncles, aunts, and in-law relatives for advice.

➔ Another co-founder said their startup had a few official advisors and another fifteen informal advisors. They met with the fifteen advisors regularly, for coffee, lunch, or dinner. These advisors were heads of other companies in the same market. They collaborated and shared information on negotiating with the channel distribution companies which distributed their products. They also talked about exit strategies: by merging some of the companies, they would create a larger property that could get a higher valuation.

➔ One founder has 30 advisors. This created an extensive network of connections to get staff, contractors, and funding. They raised all of their funding through their advisor network and didn't have to go to VCs.

Oh, and don't put Mark Zuckerberg on your advisory board without asking him.

How to Hire Staff

The purpose of staff is to help the founders with their work.

But you shouldn't hire staff in a seed startup. Your job is to develop your product and work with your customers. You must do this yourself.

If you hire staff, you create problems. You have to train them, tell them what to do, supervise them to make sure they do it, manage them when they don't do it, give them reviews, and fire them. There's also vacation schedules, sick days, birthdays, and so on. You also have pay them every two weeks so you'll need a constant flow of revenue.

You know how water won't boil if you watch it? Staffers are the opposite. Staffers won't work if you don't watch them. They'll start goofing off on the web, chat on the phone, and sneak out the back door.

When you reach 20-30 people, you have to hire HR staff. That's right, staff to take care of staff.

Just like Aeron chairs, lots of staff in a seed startup is a sign of bad management and lack of focus. Management CEOs hire a large staff so they look big.

Most seed startups never hire staff. They have only founders, advisors, and a few contractors.

➔ A friend worked at a startup that was built by a well-known Silicon Valley founder who raised $125m and hired 300 people but never developed a viable business model. The circus lasted two years.

How to Hire Contractors

You can hire contractors by the project (you pay $X for a project) or time (you pay $X for a project to be delivered in two weeks). This lets you control the costs.

Don't pay by the hour (for example, $X per hour). Startups are constantly evolving and a small project can turn into hundreds of hours. That can become very expensive.

Ask your co-founders and advisors for suggestions. Don't hire from recruiters or Craigslist because you don't know if they'll do the work. If they don't, you've lost time and money.

At first, hire the contractor on a short project to see how he performs. Look at how he does the work, how he delivers, and how he interacts with the team. Ask him to explain how he did the work.

The best SV contractors work by referral and only deal with a few clients. They won't work with clients whom they don't know or aren't friend-of-a-friend. They have ten years or more of experience and can do in a few hours what takes others two or three weeks.

Interns

No interns. Early-stage startups don't have time to train or manage interns.

Friends and Family

A startup isn't just founders. There's also a wide circle around your upstart of friends, family, girlfriends, boyfriends, and so on. This also includes everyone you meet: classmates, potential investors, potential clients, and so on.

→ Several founders use a spreadsheet to keep track of contacts. This includes name, email, phone, what they do, how you met them, who they know, and so on. They mark connections with green, yellow, or red (good, okay, bad).

Send out a newsletter every month and let them know what's going on. Invite them to parties, rollout events, speaking events, and so on. They'll tell others about your project.

That's how Twitter got started. The developers were using it for internal communication, but their girlfriends began to use it to tell each other about San Francisco parties and night clubs.

Dogs, Cats, Birds, and an Octopus

Another thing about Silicon Valley video conference calls: it's really common to see animals in conference calls. I've seen dogs, cats, hamsters, and ferrets. One guy did his calls with a bird or two on his shoulder.

I once worked with a startup that had an octopus. Octopuses can change colors and disappear into the background. The receptionist noticed if a visitor was a good person, octopus swam up to the front of the tank, but if the person was untrustworthy, octopus disappeared. The company began using the octopus as part of the hiring process.

Internal Communication

Startups evolve so rapidly that they can change direction several times in one week. This means everyone should be in constant contact.

- Seed startups are generally in contact several times every day.
- Send an internal newsletter every week to the larger team. Include a summary of what's going on and what's coming up. You can send this by email or Slack.

Discuss everything among the team: potential founders, new investors, customers, and so on. Someone may know the person or company.

→ Founders agreed that when it's small, everything is done by as a group. Everyone knows everything. Everything is done in group discussion.

→ Some founders discovered some of the co-founders didn't really understand the startup's idea. Go to each person in a private meeting and ask him to explain the project. Do this over and over until everyone understands what you're doing.

When you need an org chart, it's no longer a startup.

Another thing about communications: you must be sure everyone understands what is said. Universities teach you to speak and write academic English but that's hard to understand for many people. I've often been in meetings where the directors gave a presentation and afterwards, I asked the non-US team about it and they say they didn't really know what he was saying. It's better to talk in plain English.

Do Other Stuff

Do stuff that isn't work. That's a good way to keep your startuppyness. At various startups, we've gone hiking, canoeing, whitewater rafting, ride horses on the beach, went to the amusement park, bungee jumped, played cricket, watched movies, and went to Hawaii.

After dinner around the campfire, see if they want to talk about goals, direction, problems, and ideas. Or not.

Who Shouldn't Be a Co-founder

Some people shouldn't be in your startup:

- Students: They're busy with courses and exams. When they graduate, they're looking for jobs. Their parents will press them to take a job.
- Ex-corporate, ex-government, ex-military: Don't hire people who have worked more than three years at large organizations. They're great people, but not for startups. They're accustomed to working in structured environments but not the endless chaos of a startup. They'll come in and want to organize. You don't need organization. You need to develop product with your customers.
- MBAs: They'll try to apply methods for the management of large company. You don't need that.
- Spouses, siblings, best friends: It's very difficult to manage them or fire them. Everyone else will feel excluded. Sometimes it works, but generally not.

Look for people with experience in startups.

Visa Issues and Foreigners

If you're not a US citizen, you can get a B1/B2 visa for three or six months. Check with the US embassy in your country.

How to Make Money while Starting Up

While you're building your startup, you still need to pay the rent and buy pizza. There are several ways to do this.

Tell your advisors and professors that some of the people on your team need money. They can often put you in touch with companies that need contractors for short projects.

Often, you can take a day job that isn't too demanding. If you work part-time (three days per week or mornings), you'll have time to work on your startup. Be careful about working on your startup at work; the company may have the rights to your startup.

➜ Several founders told me they did their startups during work hours. This is more common than people realize. I know people who've done entire projects while at their day job. A few co-workers and perhaps the manager may know what you're doing. At one large company, practically every person in the engineering team was building startups. The managers knew, but that was the only way to keep them on the team.

Due Diligence

You should do due diligence (DD) on everyone who's important for your startup. "Due diligence" means you find out who they really are. Resume fraud is widespread because many people are desperate to get a job. You need to check founders, advisors, contractors, and others.

If someone tells you that he graduated in computer science from MIT, you need to be sure he actually attended MIT, studied computer science, and graduated.

There's more on DD in the chapter on Funding.

Firing People

A startup can't afford to have people in the team who don't contribute.

- Fire people who are negative. They criticize the project, the leader, the team. That's disruptive and brings down morale.
- Fire people who aren't necessary. They increase costs and time. You need to keep costs as low as possible.
- Fire people who do 100%. You need people who go above-and-beyond.
- Fire slackers. They can go to work for your competitors.

A common mistake is to hope they'll improve. When they realize they can act that way and nothing happens, they get worse. You need to remove these people immediately.

➜ Nearly every founder agreed it was hard to fire people. It's easy to fire slackers, but it's very hard to fire good people when you're running out of money. When someone gets fired, it affects the entire team. The work has to be taken up by others. The remaining team will wonder if they'll be fired and some will begin to look for other startups.

Summary: It's the Team

It's the team that counts. A lousy team with a good idea will fail. A great team can succeed with just about any idea.

➜ A VC said investors look for five things that you can count off on the fingers of your hand: the team, the team, the team, the team, and the idea.

BTW, this answers a common question about ideas. Many say if you talk openly about your idea, someone will steal it. But for anyone to do something with your idea, they have to believe in it very strongly and then build a team to implement it. That's very hard to do. Ideas are cheap. It's the team that matters.

3: Building the Company

Okay, now that we covered how to build your team, let's look at how to build the structure for your startup.

But don't get carried away with this. Focus on your team and product, not the company stuff.

Work at Home or Work at Work?

In the last few years, it has become normal to build your startup in your home. There's no point in paying rent for an office. Since the startup is a few close friends, you can do this from your home.

This also lowers your monthly expenses. For several years, Google was in a garage. Facebook was in a house a few blocks from my house. Most of the startups that I interviewed are in houses or apartments.

If you work from home, then your startup will be digital, which means a website, an email, and digital tools such as Google Suite. Your team can be anywhere in the world and you all work together online.

You could have a presence in Palo Alto. Investors and customers will take you more seriously if you're in Silicon Valley. Your development team can be in Finland and the founder team can come to SV every few months.

You can get a business address in Palo Alto. Talk with Playce.io.

Accelerators, Incubators, and Co-Working Spaces

What's the difference between accelerators, incubators, and co-working spaces?

- Accelerators: They help you to turn your idea into a viable startup in two or three months. The accelerators take equity (they get a share of your company) (about 5-7%) and give you money. At the end of the program, there's a pitch event.

- Incubators: They help you to grow your startup over one-to-two years. They generally don't give you money. They charge fees, such as $1,000 per founder per month. Some may take shares.

- Co-working Space: They give you a place to work with desks, chairs, WIFI, printers, copy machines, and meeting rooms. They often also have coffee, snacks, pinball machines, pool tables, and showers. I knew one in Palo Alto that had free beer on tap (yes, really). You pay $100 to $500 per seat per month.

All three have office infrastructure, such receptionists, conference rooms, white boards, rooms for meetings, photocopy, printers, coffee, and kitchen areas.

All of these have mentors and advisors with lots of connections. They also have private chat forums for people who've gone through the program.

At the end of the program is demo day (demonstration day), where you pitch to an audience of mostly investors. Many VC firms send scouts to look for startups. This is your big chance for funding.

Here are a few accelerators: Y-Combinator, Founders Space, IgniteXL, RocketSpace (SF), TechStars, AngelPad (SF), The Alchemist (Santa Clara), Impact Hub, Plug and Play, and Galvanize.

- Y-Combinator (YC) has two three-month sessions (Jan-Feb-Mar and Jun-Jul-Aug). Each session is one day per week for three months in Mountain View in Silicon Valley. Over 13,000 startups apply for each session but only 240 (1.8%) are accepted (it's easier to get into Stanford). They invest $120K in your startup in exchange for 7% and charge a $25K fee. They focus on startups for web and mobile but also accept others. 1,300 startups have gone through their program. On Demo Day, there are 600 investors in the audience and another 2,500 online. For more about YC, see goo.gl/n6juKf

- Founders Space (FS) is an intensive two weeks (9-5, Monday-to-Friday) in San Francisco that ends with a demo day. You have access to their advisors, mentors, and other founders for a year via their alumni group on FB. They take 3.5% of equity and they invest in some startups. Startups pay a fee to attend. If they pay more, FS takes less equity. Both the percentage of equity and the funding depends on the startup and it's negotiable. Forbes ranked it #1 for foreign startups, which is probably why 60% of their founders are foreigners. Governments often pay the fees. See FoundersSpace.com
- 500Startups has a four-month program. They invest $150K in your startup for 6% and charge a $37,500 fee. In late 2016, 500Startups said it is no longer an accelerator. They'll focus on early-stage startups.

Let's compare accelerators. The goal at YC and 500Startups is to create an investment opportunity for US funding. This means the startup must have its management in the US and be incorporated in the US. In contrast, FS educates teams how to build startups so it's okay that they set up in other countries.

YC and FS have hosted more than 1,300 startups each. Acceptance rates at YC (1.8%) and Founders Space (5%) are low because many applications are weak, so if you have a good project, you have a good chance to get in.

There are perhaps 500 accelerators worldwide and over 150 incubators and accelerators in Silicon Valley.

To find accelerators and incubators, see the National Business Incubator Association (NBIA.org) and Global Accelerator Network (GAN.co). At the NBIA, there's a list of local associations around the world (see t2m.io/4wmvhKkM). See also Angel.co and Seed-DB.com.

There are accelerators and incubators for industries, including fintech (financial technology), medicine, farming, biotech, banking, hotels, music, airlines, IoT, mobile, cars, insurance, food, real estate, and more. There are also non-profit accelerators in health, education, and minority groups. There are accelerators in Europe, Latin America, Asia, Africa, and the Middle East.

➜ If your goal is to sell your product/service (or your startup) to an industry (for example, airlines), then consider an accelerator for that industry. By joining an airlines accelerator, you get experience, connections, and visibility to people in the airline industry. That's better than a general-purpose accelerator.

Accelerators have had a significant impact on SV venture capital. From 1995 to 2005, a handful of VCs pretty much were in control of venture funding. However, when VCs got more funding, they had to get bigger successes, so they began to move up the ladder and focus only on startups that could become big.

YC was the first accelerator in 2005. At first, VCs said it wouldn't work because people wanted funding from top VCs. Y-Combinator focused on seed startups by offering both small investments (around $100K) and lots of support. By nurturing early-stage startups, YC captured the early startups that would later grow into mid-stage and late-stage startups. This gave YC power over the VCs. If VCs want to invest, they had to play nice with YC. If VCs were difficult (such as suing founders, forcing hard terms, or just being jerks), YC kept startups away from them.

To attract startups, VCs were forced to add services: mentoring, advice, financial strategy, help with staffing, and so on. They now invest in accelerators and incubators with the hope that late-stage startups will come to them.

By 2015, there were 170 accelerators. The accelerator model is evolving. 500Startups, Founders Space, and Y-Combinator and others want to become global. They are assembling worldwide networks of founders, investors, and other people.

➜ I talked with founders who went through YC or FS. They say the value is connections to experts, investors, talent, and customers. These programs are a good idea for first-time founders. Look for graduates of the programs and talk with them. Talk with the accelerator's directors and advisors to get introductions.

➜ A founder said that being in accelerators and incubators let her talk with other teams, which let her think bigger, think about what she really wanted, and clarify her vision. Another founder said the experience of being in a Silicon Valley accelerator changed everything for the project. He was in the SV environment, surrounded by other founders, advisors, and other startups, which put him in contact with investors. They showed him how to talk with investors and how to raise money.

➜ On the downside, accelerators and incubators sometimes have too much information, events, parties, or distract you from your project.

➜ Several founders said you must be proactive to get information and connections from these programs. It's up to you to reach out, learn, and make connections.

➜ Several founders used co-working spaces because their apartments were too small for a team. One said co-working spaces were all the same so they shopped around to find the cheapest one. Co-working spaces often have events. If you're not a member, you can go for $10.

To be accepted into an accelerator or incubator is a form of validation that can help in the beginning. But if you're turned down by an accelerator or incubator, it doesn't mean your idea is bad. They tend to prefer hot topics. They also give preference to apps and small, quickly developed solutions. If you're building an infrastructural platform that can take two or three years to develop, accelerators and incubators aren't the place.

Accelerators and incubators in other areas generally have less experience and connections. Look at your local accelerators and incubators and consider whether it might be better to come to Silicon Valley.

Don't join an accelerator just to join one. Pick the accelerator in the city and industry that you want. If you want to work with the US government, then go to an accelerator in Washington, D.C. But don't go there if you want to build Silicon Valley startups.

My suggestion? Look for a place with good advisors and connections to the market. Find one that works for you.

➜ One founder said they applied to many incubators and accelerators and were turned down at all of them. The team realized later that was a sign that the idea wasn't going to work.

Universities in Silicon Valley

Another idea is to go to Stanford University, University of California at Berkeley, or one of the other schools in Silicon Valley

Every summer, Stanford holds the Silicon Valley Innovation Academy (SVIA), which is an $8,000 eight-week startup course taught by Stanford professors. There are 100 students from all over the world. You live in dorms with Stanford students. This lets you meet professors, students, and the student groups for startups. Through them, you can meet angel associations for Stanford students.

UC Berkeley has Berkeley Method of Entrepreneurship Bootcamp (BMoE), a one-week intense workshop. Just as with Stanford, you meet a wide range of SV experts.

These universities also have accelerators. There is Citris Foundry at UC Berkeley Engineering. They work with engineering and biotech startups. They have a small grant ($5-10,000) and take 2% equity. This gets you into the network of professors, students, graduate students, and alumni at UC Berkeley. One member of your team must be part of UC Berkeley. Citris Foundry is setting up Blue Bear Ventures, its own investment fund.

Stanford has StartX, an accelerator for Stanford students. They also have their own investment fund. One member of your team must be part of Stanford.

There are accelerators for MIT, Harvard, and so on. Check with your school's college of engineering or computer science.

Why Set Up in Silicon Valley?

➜ One of the founders said the following about Silicon Valley: Why do mountain climbers climb Mt. Everest? If I want to climb mountains, I go walk on the hills around Silicon Valley. But if you want to be among the best mountain climbers in the world, you climb Mt. Everest.

The same with Hollywood. If you want to be in movies, you could do local movies in Berlin. But if you want to be a superstar, go to Hollywood.

The same with Silicon Valley. If you want to be the best in the world in computers and the web, then you come to Silicon Valley.

That's why Mark Zuckerberg left Harvard and came to Palo Alto. If you're serious about it, come to the Big Game. Do whatever it takes.

What If You're Not in Silicon Valley?

You don't need to live in Silicon Valley. You can keep your 20-person development team in France. Your co-founders come to SV for meetings several times a year. You can use Skype for additional meetings.

If you can, get an address in Palo Alto. It looks much better if your company is based in Palo Alto. See Playce.io.

If you're in other cities or countries, your biggest problem is your area's inexperience with startups.

Most lawyers will do legal work as if you want a large company, which means you'll pay lots of legal fees for unnecessary work. They also aren't familiar with legal issues for startups.

Accountants and financial planners will also build the financial structure for a large company. You'll pay for what you don't need.

Neither lawyers nor financial people will understand how to sell your startup.

In most countries, people have modest expectations of life and work. They don't imagine they can build a company, and certainly not if someone is only 20 years old. They'll tell you not to reach so high.

They also don't see why someone would work 60 or 80 hours per week. To them, that's irrational. They're happy with their 40-hour work weeks and six-week annual vacations.

Your family and friends will constantly offer helpful advice which will be mostly wrong. I'm from Colombia; I lived in Germany and Denmark for 15 years; I know what this is like. Pretty much most of the world thinks you should go to college and then join a large company or the government and stay there for the rest of your life.

Everyone around you (friends, family, relatives, and so on) will press you to do "the sensible thing." Your mom will want you to finish your degree. Back home, your friends and family will say, "You can't do that," "That's impossible," "You're too young to do that," "That's not the way to do that," "Wait until you have ten years of experience at a large company," "Think about your career!" and "You should settle down".

This means you'll swim against the river.

Without the advantage of their wisdom, people in Silicon Valley create companies that change the world.

➔ Many (if not all) founders said after a few weeks in Silicon Valley they never want to leave. They finally feel they're in a place where everyone understands them. They liked that people in SV help each other.

➔ Some of the founders want to move to the US because they said it is difficult to innovate in their country. They said their business culture lacked experience and knowledge. If you create something good, the large companies copy it. People want to work only at large companies so it's difficult to get good people to join startups. It's also easy to get government grants so some startups never graduate; they get one grant after another.

→ If you're building something that will be only in your country, then you should stay in your country because you'll know your market better. But if you're building for the global market, then you must come to Silicon Valley to learn how to build for that market. As I wrote earlier, 74% of SV is from other countries. Here is the only place where you'll find people with the talent and skills to build a global company.

→ Startups in Africa have to deal with additional issues. In some countries, there isn't reliable postal delivery, so companies have to build their own delivery. There's a general lack of expertise, experience, and investment capital. On the other hand, those who live there understand what works so they can develop solutions. It's nearly impossible for outside companies to enter those markets. You can't just import an idea; it has to be adapted to local conditions.

→ If your startup is incorporated outside the US, it may cause tax issues for US-based investors and VCs. Investors don't want the extra work that it will take to deal with tax issues for foreign startups, so it will become difficult (if not impossible) to get US funding for a non-US company.

When to Incorporate

Incorporation, business bank accounts, lawyers, accountants, and investors aren't in this chapter. You shouldn't deal with any of these issues until you're further in the process. After you find out that your idea can become a business, then you do those things.

For now, you only need a digital presence.

Your Startup's Digital Presence

You need to show up on the web so people can find and contact you. This is your digital presence. You only need to do just enough to show up. Don't spend too much time on this.

The bad news is that you need to build all of this at the same time. You have to set up the website, email subscription form, social profiles, buttons to the social pages, Google Ads, analytics, conversion tracking and more, all at the same time.

If this is your first time, it's a lot of work. If you've done it a bunch of times, you can do it quickly. My suggestion: bring in a contractor to set up all of this.

Your Domain Name

You have to register a domain name. but don't go to GoDaddy or any domain registrar to search for a domain name. They'll cheat you.

If you go to a registrar, find a good name for $10, go back to tell your team that you found the name, and then return to the registrar to buy it, you'll find it's now $1,000. Registrars see that you searched for the name, so they register it but they don't have to pay the $10 for 30 days. When you return, they'll offer it to you for $1,000.

To register your domain name:

- Think of a name, such as 12345.com (or whatever)
- Go to Google and enter 12345.com in the search box
- If that domain name has been registered, a website shows up or you get a page that offers to sell it to you
- If Google says, "This site can't be reached. 12345.com's server DNS address could not be found," then the domain name hasn't been registered
- Go to the domain registrar (GoDaddy and so on) and register it immediately

People have registered 325m domain names so it's very hard to get a good dot.com name. There are more than 1,300 extensions, such as .co, .ly, .app, .team, .tech, .tools, and so on (see t2m.io/Cjx4F1ta).

Your Logo

Along with a company name and domain name, you also need a logo.

You should have two logos: a temporary logo for the early-stage startup and a second, better logo for the mid-stage startup.

Because the seed startup is an experiment and you may decide it won't work or you'll pivot a few times, there's no point in spending money for a logo. You can use a temporary logo for now. Use an emoticon or a gif image. Don't pay $300. Lots of people will make logos for less than $50. Search for "design a logo." Twitter's bird logo? They paid $15 for it.

When you get a logo, be sure the sales agreement gives you all rights in all media in all countries forever.

When you grow into a mid-stage startup and you have funding, get a professional logo designer who knows how to design for all formats, such as your website, email newsletter, social media pages, Powerpoint presentations, business documents, business cards, T-shirts, stickers, and coffee cups. If you're building an app, it should also work in the app store. You'll also use your logo on large posters and six-foot banners for events and trade shows. Look at her portfolio to see if she's done this.

Digital Pages

You don't need much. You only need a few pages so people can find you and see what you're doing.

- Website: It's very easy to make a website now. Use Wordpress, Wix, SquareSpace, or similar. No HTML or code. There are thousands of free templates. If you use their URL, it's free.
- If you see a website that you like, it's likely Wordpress, so you can use WhatWPThemeIsThat.com to find out what theme they have.
- You only need three pages: About (the product), Team, and Contact. You can also put these on one long page. Add an email link and you're done. You can do this in a few hours.
- Get stock photos for your page at PixaBay.com, MorgueFile.com, Stockvault.net, EveryStockPhoto.com, FreeDigitalPhotos.net
- Another source for photos: Search at Google and select Images | Search Tools | Usage Rights | Labeled for Reuse. You can use these images.

Just so you know, it takes about twenty minutes to create a Wordpress site. Don't pay thousands of dollars for this.

If you already have a website, you can just add a page. I have my website andreas.com, so for this book, I added andreas.com/book-startup.html

You can also add your storyboard to your page as a cartoon video. It's a great way to explain what you're doing.

Social Profiles

Create a page for your startup at Facebook, LinkedIn, WeChat, and Twitter. If it's relevant, add Pinterest and Instagram. You should also create profiles for your startup at CrunchBase.com and Angel.co, which are LinkedIn for startups and Silicon Valley. In every social profile, use the same logo and message. You should show a consistent presence.

Tools

In 2005, we took the company's American Express card, went to the computer store, and spent $7,000 to set up the company. Today, it's much easier.

- Computers: Everyone has his own computer or laptop.
- Software: This is mostly free. If you show that you're a startup, Microsoft will give you Microsoft Office (Word, Excel, Powerpoint, Skype, Solitaire) and Azure cloud for free (see BizSpark at Microsoft.com). Google has Google Suite (Google Docs, Gmail, Drive, Calendar, Hangout, Frogger), Google Ads, and Analytics.
- Shared Drive: Use a shared drive so everyone can have access to files.
- Video conference calls: Skype, Hangout, or Join.me also let you share your screen. We often use all three; when one is buggy, we switch to another one.
- Cell phones. You can get a family plan for your three "cousins".
- Email Newsletter: You can send newsletters with MailChimp, Cloudy.email, ConstantContact, Sendgrid, and so on. The first 2,000 subscribers are free. I've used most of these; MailChimp is the best.
- Desks and Chairs: If you see a startup with $1,500 Aeron chairs, you know they're wasting money. When Amazon started, they went to Home Depot, got $20 doors, and put them over $10 sawhorses. You can get desks and chairs at low prices from second-hand office furniture stores. They get their furniture from startups that ran out of money.
- Slack: Use Slack for internal communication. The app also works well.
- Office supplies: Everyone buys their own office supplies.

➜ A founder had a tip for a whiteboard. Get a 4' X 8' (1/8th inch thick) melamine shower board for $12 (1.2 x 2.4 meters and 4mm thick) at large lumber supply stores (Home Depot or Lowe). Whiteboard cleaning solution is one-part isopropyl alcohol and four-parts water in a spray bottle.

Your Startup's Documents

You'll also need a business plan and Powerpoint slides for your startup. However, don't write these yet. If you write these now, you set the direction of your startup and it becomes difficult to change later. You must first do customer interviews and discover problems and solutions.

Your Website

You should add a few tools to your website.

Start by creating a new Google account. Don't use your Gmail account; others will need to log into the account and they shouldn't have access to your personal email.

- Create a Gmail account. Use a random string of letters and numbers so hackers can't guess your startup's Google email.
- Use that Gmail account to add Google Ads, Google Analytics, and Google Search Console. You should also add Bing Webmaster Tools. Add the tracking tags to your site.
- Add your credit card and turn on the Google Ads. Set up a small campaign, say, $1 per day.

Set this up as soon as possible. The various tools will start to collect keyword data.

I suggest you hire someone to set this up for you. There's a lot of configuration in the tools. It can take you several days to figure this out, several more days to fix mistakes, and then you'll have to pay someone to come in and fix the mess. Often, when I look at clients' sites, it's easier to just set up a new account. Just so you know, I can do all of this in less than an hour (but no, I won't do this for you).

Another useful thing for your website is a feedback button. Add a large button to let people send an email with feedback and suggestions. You could use a feedback widget, but an email button is easy to add and free.

Basic SEO for Startups

Okay, I've written a dozen books on SEO; I led global SEO for Cisco; I've done SEO for more than three hundred companies. Here's the red pill.

First of all, SEO is *Search Engine Optimization*, which means you optimize your webpage to show up higher in search engines. Which means you hack the search engines.

Your goal with SEO is to be findable in search engines. You can read a 500-page IBM technical book on how this works; here's the short version.

If your webpage is the official page for your company, product, or your name, it will be number one at Google and Bing.

All you have to do is to make sure that Google knows your page is the official page.

To do this, edit the TITLE and DESCRIPTION meta-tag in your website. In your product page, state the name of your product. Fill out the Contact page with full contact information: your name, your company name, your street address, email, and phone number. Add links to your Facebook, Twitter, and LinkedIn pages.

The text in meta tags appears below your URL in Google search.

Meta-tags are like tweets: you have just a few words to give the reader a good reason to click on your link.

At this point, you don't need keywords. Your name, your company name, and your product name are your keywords.

There are two meta-tags: the TITLE tag and DESCRIPTION tag.

- The meta TITLE tag is the bait to get the fish's attention. If he likes it, he'll read the DESCRIPTION line. Use up to 68 characters, including spaces. Any more may be cut off by Google. Here's an example: <TITLE>Get handmade pasta tonight | Official Site | PastaHut.com </TITLE>

- The meta DESCRIPTION tag convinces the reader that the link is what he's seeking. It starts with the main idea which is also what the customer wants. I often include the phone number, an offer ("First order is free"), and a call-to-action ("Call Now!"). Use 350 characters, including spaces. Any more may be cut off by Google. Here's an example: <meta name="description" content="Try fresh handmade pasta tonight. Artisan & organic with 000 flour. Made by hand, no machines! We make fusilli, fettuccine, linguine, penne, cannelloni, and more. For dessert, we have cannoli, zeppole, semifreddo, and more. We deliver to your door in 30 minutes. | PastaHut.com | Tel. 555.123.4567. First order is free! Call Now!"/>.

- The Meta-Keyword tag has keywords for the search engines, but Google, Bing, and Yandex no longer use it. You may ignore it.

Don't add a long series of keywords, such as "Spaghetti Pasta Lasagna Tortellini Linguini Penne." If Google notices keyword stuffing, they'll block your page. You're not adding keywords. You're writing reasons for people to visit the website.

You can do all of this yourself. Don't hire someone to do SEO.

To prove this works, I did this for my cat, Anaximander Katzenjammer. Search for his name and he's #1 at Google.

Is this really all there is to SEO? For a new startup, yes, pretty much. When you have 100,000 products and a million pages, there's more you can do, but for now, you only need a few tags.

➔ For my students at INSEEC SF, I wrote an eight-page step-by-step guide to basic SEO for startups (free at t2m.io/gHz6qxg0).

Basic Google Ads for Startups

If SEO doesn't get you to the top of Google, then you can use Google Ads (formerly known as "Google Adwords") to place your name and company at the top.

- Create one campaign with three ad groups. In one ad group, add your company name as a keyword. In the other, add your product name. If these are two words, use quotation marks around them, for example, "pasta hut." You should also include it as one word, such as pastahut (without quotation marks). In a third ad group, add your name (in quotation marks) as a keyword. Add additional ad groups for co-founders.
- Google will tell you that you need to bid $10: ignore that. Set the keyword bids to $0.25.
- Set a small daily budget of $2 per day (which will be $60 per month).
- When you set up Google Analytics, you'll get a coupon for $150 in Google Ads credit. Enter the coupon code in the billing page at Google Ads. The first $150 will be Google's money.

When you set up your account, a friendly person from Google will call and offer to set up your account.

Don't let Google do this. They give your account to high school kids who increase your budget and bids. They certainly won't set up conversion tracking for you. Each kid is managing several hundred accounts, so he doesn't care about you.

➔ I met a startup this past summer that let Google set up the account; Google spent $5,000 in one month and the startup got nothing out of it. That's how Google makes $50B per year.

Just like SEO, you don't need to do much Google Ads at the beginning.

Learn about PPC with my PPC eBook (free at t2m.io/LYOj57sx).

Keyword Research with Google Ads

Remember this morning when you installed all of those Google tools on your website? Okay, let's use that to do keyword research.

- There are lots of companies that charge money to give you keyword research data. The best keyword data is free from Google.

- In Google Ads, go to "Tools | Keyword Word Planner." In the box for "Your product or services," enter four or five of your top keywords. Under "Targeting" enter your country. Add your language. Click "Get Ideas." Google will show you additional keywords with their monthly search traffic. Sort the data by traffic and you'll see the best keywords at the top. Use those in your titles, headings, and opening sentences.

- Clear the results and this time, in the box "Your Landing Page," enter your competitor's URL. Google will show you the keywords that bring traffic to your competitor. Do this for your top five competitors. Download all five competitor results, combine them in one spreadsheet, sort them, and remove duplicates. You'll have all of the keywords for your competitors.

- In Google Ads, click the "Keywords" tab and then click the "Search Terms" button. Google will show you the keywords that people use to come to your website. Click the little down-arrow button to download the list.

- In Google Analytics, navigate to Acquisition | Search Engine Optimization | Queries. Google will show you the keywords that people used to find your site.

- In Google Search Console, navigate to "Search Traffic | Search Analytics." Google will show you yet more keywords that people used to find your site.

You're saying, wait, there are four ways to do the same thing? No. Four reports show four different sets of keywords with some overlap. Do all of these, download the reports, combine them all into a spreadsheet, and you end up with all of the keywords for your industry, along with data for each keyword.

You can do this by region (for France, India, and so on) and by language

(Spanish, German, and so on). You can also set the time scale in Google Ads to the last four years and see a graph of the volume.

The keyword report shows you the top keywords for your website, blogging, social posting, tweets, and so on. Give the keyword report to your investors. It shows whether there's a market for your product.

This is why you must install the Google tools as soon as possible so the tools can start to collect data. If you don't do this, it'll be bad. How bad? Here are two stories.

Once upon a time I worked with a startup that built their company in the olden ways of their fathers' fathers from lands far away. They raised a million dollars, hired ten engineers, hired sales and marketing people, web designers, an office mom, and several interns. They spent 18 months but they hadn't yet talked with a customer. I join the circus and after a few days, I did a keyword review. I printed out the top keywords, along with the monthly search traffic. At the weekly team meeting, I handed this out. The top keyword for their industry has 1,400 searches worldwide per month. That was it. My cat's webpage gets more traffic than that. The CEO looked at the list and his face had the same look as when you stood on that tiny platform for your first bungie jump. Or when you faced your first wife's divorce lawyer. Remember that? That bad. There was no market. The company was dead six months later.

Let's end this section on a happy note. Okay, there's death in it, but it's California so it's happy anyway. I'm working with a large cemetery. Yes, they need marketing too. They want to sell more graves. Among other things, I do a keyword report. The night before a meeting, I prepare the list and I notice there were a lot of searches for "bury my dog," "bury my cat," and so on. I thought, if I go to the meeting with that, they'll think I'm crazy, so I took out the animal searches. But then I thought, wait, that's data, so I put it back in and went to the meeting.

The meeting was what you'd expect: a bunch of people in dark suits and ties. I'm presenting and we're talking so I get to the keyword report and I hand out copies. I explain the report and we discuss the keywords. And then I say, "You may notice, at line 32 there's a lot of searches to bury dogs and cats." One of the VPs slams his fist on the table and says, "I knew it! I knew there a market for pet burials!" A few months later, they call me up and say to come over and see. They created a small park for pet burials and it was nearly full. See? By looking at the data, they discovered a market and people were happy.

Use Google Ads to Find a Name for Your Product

You can use keyword research to find a name for your company and product. Do the keyword research and look for words with lots of monthly searches.

Use Google Ads to Test Your Idea

You can also use Google Ads to test your idea. You can launch ad campaigns for something that doesn't exist to see if people come to the website. Set up a subscribe button to collect names and emails.

Set Up the Newsletter

You should also send a monthly email newsletter to keep your team, advisors, investors, clients, and friends updated. They'll tell others what you're doing.

Send a monthly newsletter to your customers. Update them on your progress. Ask for feedback and suggestions. When someone writes to you, don't send automated replies. Write a personal reply.

You can use email tools such as MailChimp, Cloudy.email, Sendy, Constant Contact, and others.

Add a newsletter subscribe button to your website. The email tools give you a bit of code to put a Subscribe link on your website to ask people to subscribe to your newsletter.

It may sound nice to have 50,000 subscribers, but what counts are the ones who actually read your newsletter. If someone hasn't opened your newsletter in the last three months, they're not interested and you should delete them from your subscriber list.

You'll have to download the emails of your contacts in Facebook, LinkedIn, Gmail, and so on. To do that:

- **Gmail:** Click Gmail (red button, far left). Select Contacts. Click More. Select All Contacts. Save as CSV.
- **LinkedIn:** Go to LinkedIn | Click My Network | Connections (top, middle). Click the gear icon (far right). Click on Export LinkedIn Connections (right column). In the "Export to:" dropdown menu, select Microsoft CSV.

- **Facebook:** Create a Yahoo email account. Go to address.yahoo.com, click the Facebook icon. Sign in with your Facebook ID. This imports your Facebook address book to your Yahoo Mail account. Go to Yahoo | Tools | Import. Export as CSV or press Control + A to Copy All and paste in a text file.

You can also scan business cards with a business card scanner. You can also use smart phone apps which take photos of business cards and convert the image to text.

Combine all of the emails into one list and remove duplicates. Next, scrub the list. Many email addresses are abandoned each year so you need to delete the bad emails. If you don't scrub, you'll get hundreds of bounced emails, your email host may think you're a spammer, and they'll shut down your account.

To scrub, use DataValidation.com, which is about $7 per 1,000 email addresses. You upload your list of email addresses and after a few days, it gives you a list with the emails marked as Good, Maybe, or Bad. Send emails to the Good and Maybe. Delete the bad emails.

All of your co-founders should do this with their Gmail, Facebook, and LinkedIn email accounts to create a large list.

Don't send bulk emails from your Gmail account. If you send more than 300-400 per day, Google may shut down your account. If this is the account for your project, you'll have to start all over again.

What about Revenue, Marketing, and Other Stuff?

Many startups make two fatal mistakes:

- Product in Search of a Market: They build a product first and then try to find a market for it. Webvan was a billion-dollar startup without a market.
- Strong Marketing to Fix a Weak Product: They have a poor product so they do lots of marketing to sell it.

The easy solution is to raise a bunch of money for sales and marketing to create sales, which is what investors want to see. VCs secretly like that because they're paid to give you money.

Don't get me wrong: marketing works… for large companies. I've done this for global corporations. But they do things that are far beyond what startups can do.

Several people pointed out to me that advertising is the tax that you pay when your product isn't good.

Marketing is like the use of steroids to cover up weak muscles.

You shouldn't be doing marketing and sales in an early-stage startup. If you do, you'll get tied up in that and you won't do development. You should finish the product before you start sales. Make products that users love. That'll grow virally.

Anyway, since you're probably wondering, I added a bunch of stuff for mid-stage startups to my blog about this.

- How to build branding
- How to test your logo, colors, fonts, and website
- How to use the newsletter for testing
- How to get new customers and keep your customers
- How to get reviewers to review your product.
- How to use Google for advertising
- How to use ASO for apps
- Social media marketing, content marketing, and growth hacking
- How to get in magazines and newspapers
- How to speak at conferences and tradeshows
- And other stuff

Summary

The point of digital presence is to show up when people look for you. They want to see who you are and what you've done. This includes potential co-founders, advisors, customers, and investors. Make sure people can find you online.

4: Interview Your Customers

Before You Develop Your Product

Before you start writing code, incorporate, or order your T-shirts, you should find out if there's a market for your idea.

Key Idea: You do this by interviewing your customers. How do they do their work? Where are their frustrations? How much does that problem cost them? What would solve that problem? How do customer find out about solutions? If you do this well, your customers will tell you what they need, how much they'll pay, and how they'll buy it.

After you have ten or twenty interviews, you will have a good idea of what to develop.

Your Customers and Your Company

One of the most important parts of your company are your customers because they pay you. You need to understand what your customers do, what's broken, and how to fix it.

➔ At the beginning of your startup, you should spend 80% of your time on customers and 20% on development. As time goes by, this slowly flips to 20% time on customers and 80% on development. Of course, this depends on the industry. This isn't possible with large, complex projects such as programming languages, complex medical devices, large industrial machines, and so on.

➔ This goes further than just knowing your customers; you need fall in love with your customers. Learn everything you can about your customers; what they like, how they do things. This is why meetings with customers should be in person where possible, and if not, then via Skype video chat. You need to see what makes them happy, what causes hesitation, and what they avoid. Learn to see your customers' business from their point of view.

How to Interview Your Customers

You interview your customers to learn about their work and life so you can develop a better product for them.

The next few sections are based in part on Rob Fitzpatrick's short book *The Mom Test*. It's a great little book and you should get it. See MomTestBook.com.

This isn't just theory. To write this book, I interviewed founders, VCs, angels, investors, and heads of incubators, accelerators, and co-working spaces. I asked them to tell me how they built their startups, what works, what doesn't work, what they do, and what they don't do. I used those interviews to write this book. That's why this book is hands-on reality.

The interviews caused me to rethink large parts of this book. Many sections were rewritten, deleted, or expanded, based on what founders told me about their startups.

How to Find People for Interviews

Reach out to everyone:

- Friends, family, college classmates, and alumni
- Co-founders, advisors, co-workers
- Professors at universities and business schools
- Investors
- People who sign up for your newsletter or register at your website

➜ One founder said you must also interview failed startups. Look in Angel.co and other sites for founders to find similar startups.

➜ One of the interviewed founders is a student, so she said she was doing research for a student project, which was mostly true.

➜ You should also interview potential investors. A founder discovered that one of Silicon Valley's leading angels had lost $26m the previous year in the startup's target market. All of the other angels knew about this so none were willing to invest.

How Many Interviews?

➜ I asked founders how many interviews they had done. One did 70 interviews over two months. Three did 30 interviews. Most did 10 to 20 interviews. One founder used 800 surveys and another used 1,500 surveys. Some didn't interview anyone. I interviewed 26 people for this book.

Example of an Email

Here's an example of an email that you can send: Dear Bob; I'm developing a product for the construction industry. I'm trying to understand how your industry works. You have lots of experience and that could help me avoid mistakes. I'm not selling. I just want to learn. Can I buy you lunch and talk about this? – Emily

➜ For this book, I sent an email to the 1,500 subscribers of my personal newsletter. About 45 replied and I interviewed 26 of them.

Before the Interview

You should know who you are interviewing. Prepare for the interview by researching the person and his company. Look at his website, Facebook, Twitter, LinkedIn, Instagram, and so on. Look at his education, career history, and personal interests. Look at his company's website and LinkedIn page. Look for news stories about the company (go to Google News and search for him and the company.)

Who Should Do the Interviews

You and your co-founders should be doing interviews. You can't outsource this or hire students to interview for you. You must do this yourself.

Each interview should be done by a pair of co-founders. Don't send the same two people to every interview.

How to Do the Interview

- Make sure he understands this isn't a sales call. You're talking with him because he's an expert.
- Send the questions before the interview so he can prepare.

- Don't present your project. Don't talk about your project. Just ask questions. Let him talk.
- Bring two copies of questions on paper. Give him a copy.
- Record the interview. This lets you focus on the conversation instead of taking notes. There are apps to record phone calls and conversations.
- Don't interview in offices; that's too formal and he won't talk openly. Don't interview in crowded coffee houses because others may overhear and he won't talk openly. Don't sit with a desk or table between you. Sit at the end, side by side.
- Don't be formal. Be relaxed and chat.

If you use video chat, turn on the video so you can see each other. Face expressions tell you a great deal.

The Wrong Questions

Many customer interviews ask the wrong questions. They demonstrate the product and then ask the customer if he will buy the product.

The result is an opinion ("yes, maybe") but that doesn't help you because when you talk, you don't learn anything. You learn by listening.

Polls, surveys, or multiple-choice questionnaires will miss details and problems. Ask open-ended questions and let them talk.

➜ Don't assume customers are all alike. A startup was developing a medical device so they interviewed doctors. The expert doctors asked for advanced features so these were added, but the tool became too complex for normal doctors, so sales fell. Expert users are often too advanced for the broad market.

Questions to Ask

Key Idea: Ask specific questions about the customer's past actions. What was the problem? Why did it matter? How much did it hurt? What did he do about it?

For example, you're building an app for a construction company. Here are ideas for the kinds of questions that you can ask:

- How are you currently doing this process? Talk me through step-by-step the last time you did this process.

- What part of the process has problems?
- Are there problems with the tool?
- What other tools did you try before you chose the tool that you use?
- How are you dealing with the problem now?
- How would you fix it? Very often, they really know the problem and they'll tell you how to solve it.
- Why haven't you fixed this?
- Is it really a problem or do you just put up with it?
- What are you really trying to do? What's the real point of all this?
- Are you looking for a replacement?
- What stops you from replacing the tool?
- Where do you look for replacements?
- Who do you listen to when you look for replacements?
- How much money are you losing because of the tool?
- Is there a budget for a better tool?
- Who controls the budget for new tools?
- What's the process to select new tools?
- What's the name of the person who makes the decisions?
- Who else should I talk with?
- What else should I ask?

The last question is important. People will tell you stuff that you didn't consider.

To give you options, I listed too many questions. Use this list to make your own questions. Aim for about 10-12 questions for about an hour of conversation.

➔ One of the founders told me that the team asked questions about the user's situation, just as I described above. I asked why they did it that way and they said because their professor told them to ask questions, but they didn't have a product, so they just asked people about problems. That led them to discover a problem and then develop a product to solve that problem.

Keep Asking Questions

→ Several founders had another way to ask questions. One team added online chat to the product. People contacted the company for support and after the problem was fixed, he asked them questions. Generally, they answered.

→ Another team offered 24/7 online chat for their worldwide customers. The co-founders, even after running the company for four years, made a point of doing 30 minutes of chat support every day to stay in touch with their customers. They ask customers and got lots of feedback and suggestions.

After the Interview

Put the interview material (your summary, the video, audio recording, and photos of your written notes) on a shared drive. Everyone on the dev team should have access to the interviews.

Each co-founder should read all of the interviews. Next, get the team together and discuss each interview, one by one. What's good, what should be developed, what doesn't matter.

Apply the Interviews to Your Development

Hold a team meeting to discuss each interview, line by line. What new information is there? How can you apply the new information to your product dev? How does it change your product, development, and future of the project?

Convert the Interviews into a Storyboard

When you have a clear understanding of the customers' problem, you create a storyboard.

A storyboard is a description of the process from the user's point of view. What he's doing, the problem that happens, how it affects his work, and how it can be fixed.

A storyboard can be in several forms:

- A few paragraphs
- An outline with numbered steps

- A cartoon drawing of stick figures with text in bubbles and subtitles
- A video with animated cartoon characters

The storyboard should be short. By keeping it short, you state the problem/solution quickly and clearly. This means a half page of text, one page of drawings, or a 30-second video.

You can make different versions of the storyboard for different audiences:

- For your development team
- For your investors
- For customers on your website

There are plenty of webpages and blogs where you can see how to write storyboards. You can see how Jake Knapp at Google Ventures does rapid prototyping with storyboards (see t2m.io/XvpjBVLG).

➜ Nearly all of the interviewed founders wrote storyboards and found these useful.

➜ A few didn't use storyboards. They felt this was just an exercise. They had lots of experience in the issue and a clear understanding of their customers and market so they didn't need to write a storyboard.

➜ Several founders said the investors weren't interested in the interviews or storyboards. They said investors don't have much time. The investors only cared about financial issues.

The Problem with Asking Questions

You ask questions to clear up doubt and confusion. What do you get? More doubt and confusion.

If you ask ten professionals, you'll get ten answers.

When you look at all of the interviews and summarize them, you may discover a few common positions and problems.

➜ One founder used interviews, but realized there were problems with interviews. If you had asked people five years ago about on-demand car services, they would have said they use taxi. They didn't imagine Uber.

Learn to Listen

It's hard to hear what people tell you. You want confirmation of your ideas, not more issues.

I started this book with the idea that startups should be built with metrics. Everything should be tested so you collect the data, apply statistics, and discover the optimal solution.

➜ I talked about metrics with three founders who had strong engineering skills and had done multiple startups. They all said, "Well, yeah… we tried that, but it didn't really work out." I thought they hadn't done it right. Yes, I ignored their experience. My theory was better.

Finally, I realized what they were saying: metrics-based development doesn't work. Many leading books on startups talk about metrics, but they don't explain how to actually do this because it doesn't work.

Write Your Startup's Documents

After you've finished with customer interviews, you'll have a clear idea of the problem and solution. Now you can write your startup's documents:

- One-pager: Your business summary on one page.
- Ten-page pitch deck: These are ten slides in Powerpoint and PDF for investor presentations.

You can download templates for the one-pager and the ten-page pitch deck at this book's webpage which you can edit for your startup. There are hundreds of business plans at BPlan.com.

Put these documents on a shared folder that everyone in your team can use. You can also put them on a small USB drive on your keychain and in a folder on your phone's memory.

Practice these over and over until you can present them with confidence.

➜ Many of the founders with lots of experience don't write 10-page or 60-page business plans. You'll spend too much time on that. Everything will change so much so quickly that it'll be obsolete within a few weeks. Many investors won't read it or they just skim it. Everyone knows it will change anyway, so this can be a waste of time.

Your Elevator Pitch

The elevator pitch got its name because you presented your idea while riding an elevator from one floor to another.

But most elevator pitches are long awkward sentences such as "we leverage dynamic verticals." Nobody knows what that really means and nobody cares.

At a pitch event, someone went on for two minutes about storage and sharing of bio data in the enterprise cloud space until one of the investors said, "You're doing medical records?"

A better solution is the grandmother pitch.

Your Grandmother Pitch

Key Idea: Your grandmother pitch is something that your grandmother will say about your startup to my grandmother.

Write your pitch and then turn it into three or four plain words that your grandmother would say. It has to be spoken words, not a written sentence. I call this the grandmother pitch.

- Talk with your grandmother and ask her what she thinks you're doing. If she says "You're wasting your time on that Gameboy! Get a real job!", then you know she's honest. When she says "Little Johnny makes it easy to pay people," you have a good phrase.

- You know you have a good grandmother pitch when people introduce you to other people and they use your phrase. "Jenny, I want to you to say hello to Johnny. He makes it easy for people to pay other people."

- By saying it in simple words, it becomes easy for people to say it to other people. That gives it virality.

In Silicon Valley, we call these "X for Y" statements. It's this for that. The X is a well-known large company that everyone understands what it does. The Y is a noun that everyone also understands. For example, it's AirBnB for parties. Facebook for dogs. LinkedIn for cats. If you run out of ideas, try ItsThisForThat.com :-)

See more about the Grandmother Pitch at t2m.io/CfoPSknM

Use Google Ads to Test Your Grandmother Pitch

When you have several pitch phrases to describe your startup, you can test them in Google Ads to find the best one.

- Create an ad group in Google Ads.
- Use only one keyword. Use a relevant keyword that has the most traffic.
- Create ads for each grandmother pitch. If you have five phrases, make five ads. Everything should be the same, just the body of the ads should be different. Put the pitch message in the body of the ad.
- Turn off ad optimization. Set this to ad rotation.
- Run the ads in a week without major holidays until you have 1,000 impressions for each ad. Look at the ad's CTR (click-through-rate) to pick the best ad.
- You'll see which one gets the most clicks.

You need 1,000 impressions per ad to get +/-3% statistical confidence.

How to Get Your First Customers

Your first customers are of course your own team. You start dogfooding to see if your own team will use your product. Google tests products extensively on their own employees before release.

Next are the people around your startup. These include advisors, contractors, investors, and so on. Give them the product to try.

Finally, give the product to people whom you interviewed.

Start with a small group. You want enough to give you feedback, but not so much that you spend too much time in customer support. Don't worry about revenue in the beginning. Offer the first few versions for free or a small fee. At this point, feedback and exposure is more valuable.

Use digital ads in Google Ads and Facebook to reach your audience. Send them to your website where they can register, sign up for your newsletter, or download your product.

Your customers will tell others about your product. Ask for testimonials. Ask them to post photos and videos to your website, your Facebook page, their website, and their Facebook page.

What if you can't get customers? It may be that you didn't clearly state your tool's benefit so you need to explain it better.

But if you still don't get customers, then people are telling you they don't need your product.

→ Several founders said they got lists of potential customers and called them. This may or may not work, but you'll only know if you try. Get a list of 100 customers, call them, and see if that works.

More Ideas

You don't need an original idea. If you're in Europe, South America, Asia, or Africa, look at successful SV startups and see if those ideas will work in your country.

That actually works. The Sanwer brothers of Austria make copies of SV companies for Europe. They even copy entire websites. They hire teams to manage the copies. Their company is worth a billion dollars.

Look for SV companies that got investors and have lasted more than three years. They've figured out what works (and doesn't work). See if you can improve the idea for your country and make it better.

Two of the largest companies in the world are Baidu and Alibaba in China; both are copies of Silicon Valley companies; both are worth billions of dollars. Google itself is a copy of someone else's work.

Don't build a startup to make money from advertising. Most online media sites actually make very little. My blog has data on ad revenue (go to andreas.com/blog-2014.html and search for "Adsense").

Yet More Ideas

Still don't know where to start?

There is an explosion of new technologies. These will create platforms, companies, tools, and service companies. Look at IoT (Internet of Things), AI, machine learning, robotics and drones, 3D printing, blockchain, CrispR, augmented reality, and virtual reality. Each one of these will create billion-dollar companies.

Drs. Carl Benedikt Frey and Michael Osborne at the University of Oxford estimate 47% of jobs can be automated (see t2m.io/Rg9QPnzF for a list of 702 occupations at p. 57-72).

You can build startups to automate these jobs. Look for companies where they still work on paper. Pick an occupation, interview people to learn its inefficiencies, and develop a better solution. Find a hole and fill it.

Good Development Goes Viral

Viral distribution, viral marketing, virality, and the network effect are several words for the same thing: people tell others, who tell others, and it grows on its own, which means it goes viral.

There are two kinds of virality:

- Emotional virality. Something that appeals to either positive or negative emotions can grow very fast. After it peaks, it collapses quickly. Examples are Pokémon and Susan Boyle.

- Utility virality: If it solves a problem for the user, he'll share with friends and each friend will share with more friends. This starts slowly and grows quickly. Because it's useful, people will use it for a long time. The best example is email.

Another example of virality based on utility was Dialpad. In 1998, Dialpad offered the first free web-based long-distance calling. This was before Skype. It was the fastest-growing website in history and became one of the top sites on the web. I was the head of digital marketing at Dialpad. Nobody had ever seen viral growth so we didn't know why it was growing so fast. It grew because it allowed people to talk long distance worldwide for free.

Professors at Stanford, Wharton, Copenhagen, and other places have studied why things go viral. At my blog, there's a collection of academic research articles in viral marketing (see t2m.io/LShn8AmY).

Build Virality into Your Product

You can increase virality by first building a product that solves a problem.

Next, tell your users the benefit in crystal-clear words. Don't let them figure it out or guess. You can test these messages with Google Ads.

Finally, make it easy for your customer to tell others. Add click-to-share buttons for Facebook, Twitter, and so on. Build a list of customers who like your product. Add a monthly newsletter with MailChimp.

Reduce any barriers to sharing. Funny cat videos go viral because you only have to copy a Youtube URL. If new users have to fill out a registration form and confirm the password, fewer will sign up.

You can increase virality by offering a referral coupon. If the new user signs up, she gets a 10% discount. You can use "double-loop referral" (yes, it's a bad name) where both the sender and recipient get a referral coupon. If I invite you to use Uber, you get a free ride and I also get a free ride.

Videos also work well. Make short two-to-three minute videos of yourself with your product that show the benefit to the user. Post these in Youtube, your website, and all of your social media profiles.

What If It Doesn't Go Viral?

If it doesn't go viral, your users don't see the value in your product. This means you'll have to use sales and marketing. Marketing convinces people to buy stuff they don't need.

Does Marketing Really Work?

Whiners say marketing doesn't work. Folks, it works. The trillion-dollar luxury consumer market exists because of marketing.

If you can't get the product to go viral, bring in experienced marketing people. They can find an audience and create demand.

➔ Marketing depends on the country. What can be used in one country often isn't possible in another country. For example, Google and Facebook work in the US but not in China. The Google Play app store also doesn't work in China. Instead, there are third-party app stores that connect to users via social networks such as WeChat, where stores have created pages like magazines to talk about games.

What about Metrics and KPIs?

Metrics and KPIs won't help in your seed startup phase. You need to interview customers, discover a problem, develop a solution, and get the initial investors.

➜ Some investors want a weekly metrics report. They don't realize it can take two or three hours to prepare reports, an hour to deliver, and another hour for follow-up. There are only 100 work hours in a week, so you're spending 5% of your week on something that doesn't add value. Explain that to the investor and see if he'll accept a monthly metrics report.

Summary

It's amazing how many companies crash because the founders and investors build products without talking with their customers. They think they know their market. This happens over and over in Silicon Valley.

Talk with potential customers. Ask them what they do and what problems they face. They're frustrated and they'll tell you. That gives you the opportunity to build solutions.

The rest of your work is easy: solve that problem, develop a prototype, and test it to see if it really solves the problem. Investors will fund your project.

These solutions work because they fit an existing market. Just fix the problem.

5: Develop Your Product

Traditional Startups

From the 1960s to the early 2010s, Silicon Valley startups were mini-companies. What did that mean? Starting in the early 1990s, I worked at perhaps three dozen startups where we built companies: we rented office space, set up cubicles, hired sys admins, bought servers, hired sales, marketing, receptionists, and HR. We did production, warehousing, marketing, sales, distribution, and transactions. There was also support, returns, repairs, and so on. All of this was done by ten to twenty people. These small companies did the same functions as a large company so we were busy.

All of this started to change in the late 2000s.

Lean Startups as Experiments

Steve Blank wrote *The Four-Steps to the Epiphany* (2005). It was followed by *The Lean Startup* by Eric Ries in 2011. Steve Blank also wrote *The Startup Owner's Manual* (2012).

These books changed how we understand Silicon Valley startups. They pointed out that a startup shouldn't be a company. Instead, a startup should be a process to discover if an idea can become a business. Early-stage startups should focus on product development. They should not do revenue activities such as marketing and sales.

Is this Theory or Does It Really Work?

Blank and Ries' books write that you should get out of the building and talk with customers, which is what I did by interviewing founders.

→ I interviewed founders for this book. I asked about the idea of lean startup and Eric Ries' *Lean Startup* book. Three founders had read Ries' book. Two skimmed it. Some had the book but never read it. Most didn't know about it. Most had heard the concept of lean startups and could describe it in a few sentences, which mostly included MVP (minimal viable product). Most did several customer interviews. Most built and launched their products on their feeling it would work.

➜ This included startups with funding. Investors generally use the North Korean missile strategy: build, launch, and pray. Some investors did research, but most didn't. The investors felt the idea would be good. Some investors carried out due diligence of founders, but not the product or market. Their research mostly a traditional MBA search for the size of the market (revenues, number of users) and ranking of competitors.

➜ In general, founders said most investors didn't understand or care about metrics. They only wanted metrics for growth and revenues. They ignored other metrics. Some investors didn't understand network effect. A few said that monthly metrics report reassured investors that the startup was keeping track of progress.

➜ A founder with many years of experience said most startups don't try to solve problems. They build something and then look around to see what it can solve and who'll pay for it.

➜ Another founder knew the various lean startup books. He said they tried to apply these but it didn't work. Build-measure-learn doesn't give you a direction nor tells you what to do. The danger is that if you start off in the wrong direction, build-measure-learn will let you optimize in the wrong direction and once you begin to follow a path, it's nearly impossible to get out of it.

➜ Many of the founders told me they hadn't read any books or had a startup strategy. They just jumped into it. The founders on their third or fourth startup didn't think about it. They had an idea from customers and just started. Some had tried to develop with metrics, but couldn't see how to apply it.

➜ Another founder is building a platform. We talked about lean startup and they knew the concept, but said it didn't apply to them. If you're building a tool or app, you can build prototypes, test them with users, and get feedback. But for infrastructure (say, a new programing language), you can't test a partial tool. Users have to understand the technology and its application before they can give feedback. Only advanced developers can do that.

➜ Several founders said that in manufacturing or medical devices, each production cycle can take six to twelve months and costs several hundred thousand dollars, so you can't just try something and then throw it away.

They also found they couldn't get meaningful feedback from most users about complex products. You need to spend weeks or months with a handful of expert specialists to get useful feedback.

➜ I asked founders about metrics. One founder with ten years of experience was on his third funded startup and admitted it was only six months ago that he heard about KPIs. Several founders didn't use any metrics. They relied on experience and gut feeling.

➜ One founder said that metrics works very well for small software products for web and mobile, such as gaming, because these get lots of users quickly so you can get lots of data and make changes. Gaming is a numbers game. You can get data on users, daily traffic, retention, churn, in-game payments, revenue per customer, and so on.

➜ Another founder told me that he was using KPIs for sales, but not for development. His team had tried to develop KPIs so they could give bonus for the quality of code or the speed of work, but they couldn't solve that problem.

➜ Most of the first-time founders were overwhelmed with learning how to set up everything, including co-founders, talking with customers, developing products, incorporation, lawyers, funding, and so on. They have no time for tests or metrics.

➜ Several founders said most startup books were generally written by successful, wealthy founders ("How I Became a Billionaire in Four Days" or whatever) so those books don't talk about what it's really like for everyone else. Most founders experience a great deal of frustration, doubt, and isolation.

➜ By the way, many of the founders under 25 said they never read books. At all. They read blogs or listen to podcasts (which means I will post sections of this book as blog articles and audio).

➜ I also interviewed the heads of accelerators. Founders Space has hosted over 1,300 startups in many fields. They said there is no general strategy for startups. Every startup is unique and has its own situation to solve. It depends on the team, location, technology, industry, and so on.

Blank and Ries' core idea is good: startups aren't miniature companies. Startups are a process to discover a viable business. The idea to "get out of the building", which means to learn what customers actually do, is also good. The rest of it isn't useful.

Product Dev into Six Bullet Points

It's pretty simple:

- Interview your customers to find the problems that cost them time or money (this is covered in the next chapter).
- Write a storyboard of the problem and solution.
- Convert the storyboard into code.
- Show investors that customers have a problem and your solution will save time and money. They'll give you funding to build the company.
- With funding in hand, you incorporate and take care of the legal stuff.
- Your customers will tell others about your product because it saves them time and money. You'll grow virally.
- You switch from seed startup into a mid-stage startup where you focus on growing the business, which means you build marketing and sales, get customers, and handle revenue.

Build a founder team that talks with customers to discover their problems and develop products that solve those problems.

What You Should Not Do

Don't do this in your early-stage startup:

- Don't build a large team. When you add production, staff, marketing, sales, customers, and bureaucracy, it becomes harder to change. Those activities take up time and work, which means you aren't developing the product.
- Don't chase growth. You'll be under strong pressure from investors to grow. Early-stage startups need to develop the product, not grow.
- Don't chase money. If you bring in investors just for the money, they may not be aligned with your goals. They'll insist on revenues and users, which will distract from development.
- Don't bring in MBAs to do business strategy. They're trained to manage large companies so they'll apply large company methods to your two-founders-and-a-cat startups. This includes methods such as customer profiles, SWOT, market analysis, business development, quadrants, and TAM (Total Addressable Market, which means how much money there is). This distracts from what you should be doing

and creates analysis paralysis. Seed startups evolve so fast that 60-page business strategies are obsolete within a week. (BTW, if investors want to know TAM, do a quick search for "2016 revenues in _____ (insert your market)" and make them happy.)

You can do all of these things after you've developed a great product. You sell the startup for $10m to a large company and they bring in a tall, silver-haired CEO with a monosyllable first name followed by a dog pack of Ivy-League MBAs. Let them wreck the company. You take your $10m and move on to your next startup.

➔ Many founders told me you have to be able to develop the technology yourself. That's the only way to truly understand your market and product. By developing the product by hand, from the ground up, you see how to do it better. In some cases, you can hire contractors, but you have to understand what they are doing. One startup hired a company to build its website, sales platform, and database. After three months, they had no sales. They added a database advisor who reviewed the code and found the database was fake. That mistake nearly killed the company.

➔ Founders also told me that investors ask if you can develop the technology. One was asked, "Why are you the ideal team to develop this idea?" Show that you have the knowledge, skills, and experience to do it.

Stay Foolish. And Small.

Along with Steve Job's "stay foolish," you should stay small as long as possible. This lets you build a better product.

When your startup is just a few people, you can pivot quickly. I'm working with a startup that pivoted three times in four days.

By the way, *pivot* is French and it means "to turn." Just a fancy way to say you change direction.

➔ Pivot is a good thing. As your team learns more about your customers and market, you'll have lots of great ideas. When you have an idea that's better than your project, switch to that. As for the other great ideas, write them down for your next startup.

➔ Don't be afraid to pivot. Startup people love to build products. They put time, emotion, and work into the product and after a while, they don't want to hear feedback. They stop listening.

→ This is a common problem at accelerators: when many startups join an accelerator, they've already gone down the development path, so the product is set. If it's not the best idea or there are problems, they don't want to hear it and it's hard to pivot. At the very beginning of the project, before it's been defined, there is more possibility for evolution. The less has been done, the more opportunity for improvement.

What to Build

Companies prefer not to innovate or compete. It's much easier to just sell an existing product that makes money. The staff only has to do the same work every day. As long as money comes in, they won't change.

Processes are generally developed until they're good enough for the market. This means there is lots of inefficiencies within companies. If you uncover an inefficient process and the cost is great enough, you can build a solution.

You could be disruptive or build a brilliant new thing, but that's difficult and not likely. It's easier to fix existing problems. Companies will buy because you save them time and money. With the web, you can reach a global market.

Is There a Market for Your Product?

Product/market fit (PMF) is an awkward way of asking if the market will buy the product.

It's all very nice to make dog food that dog owners will buy, but the owners aren't your audience. It's the dog. Will the dog eat the dog food?

It seems obvious, but building a product without researching the market is common. People in Silicon Valley are very smart so they think they know what the market wants. "Build it and they will come" sometimes works, but mostly no. Webvan, Iridium, and many more were billion-dollar disasters.

CBInsight looked at 101 failed startups and found the leading causes of death were no market need (42%), ran out of money (29%), and not the right team (23%). Running out of money happens because there was no market need, poor product, or a failure to evolve.

➜ Most startups don't validate their business before they start developing. They get excited about doing a startup and they dive into development. Six months of development go by, they're ready to start sales, and they discover there is no market.

➜ Don't get into a market where one company can shut you down. Founders told me they had built apps and a year later, one of the big companies released a free app that copied their app. Other developers build copy-cat ad-based free versions.

➜ An investor told me that startups don't die on their own. They're killed by founders who won't work hard, won't learn, or the founders make critical mistakes, such as building products without a market.

Summary: What's with the Cover?

You may wonder about the cover of this book. I went to bookstores, magazine racks, and libraries and looked at hundreds of images. I looked at many more images on the web. I looked at book covers on Amazon. We developed perhaps fifteen designs for the cover.

It has to be something about startups, but what do you see when you talk about startups? A bunch of people in a small office? But startups aren't done in small offices anymore. Everyone works from home.

A drawing of someone at a computer with a cat on her lap? I'd get so many angry emails from dog lovers, bird lovers, ferret lovers, and an octopus or two (yes, that happens. I once did an illustration for software that featured a girl bee. Some guy wrote an angry email that this was anti-male sexism.)

Several ideas for covers were professional, like something by IBM, but when I showed them to founders in their early 20s, they said those looked like something by IBM.

What are startups? When you start, only a few people understand and it changes over and over. It's chaotic creativity, so I began to look at abstract expressionism.

What about the letters on the cover? A startup isn't a thing; the product is the thing. You don't see the startup; you see the product. That's why I cut away the letters to make holes.

Maybe this makes sense to you. Maybe not. Whatever. Turn the page.

6: Legal Stuff

The rest of this book is stuff about legal issues, funding, accounting, finances, and so on. Yes, boring stuff.

You should do this stuff only as little as necessary. Don't get caught up in this. Focus on getting to know your customers and build great product.

You need to fix the legal stuff before you get funding. So…lawyers first, followed by money (it's usually the other way around).

To summarize this chapter in one sentence, you incorporate your company so you can give stock to your team, investors can give you money, and you can sell the company.

All of the numbers in this chapter are just examples. Even the page numbers are examples. All money numbers are in US dollars. Your actual numbers may be different.

First, a Word from My Lawyer and My Cat

This chapter isn't legal advice. I'm not a lawyer. I'm giving you an overview of some legal issues for startup founders. I won't be liable for any loss including without limitation, indirect or consequential loss or damage. This information may not be correct, complete, or up-to-date. Talk with your lawyer.

Don't ask my cat for legal advice. He's not a lawyer. He's a cat.

How to Choose a Lawyer

The first question is what kind of lawyer do you want? One of the big law firms, such as Wilson-Sonsini or Fenwick & West, or a small law firm?

It'll look prestigious if your lawyer is at a big law firm. They handle the big boys, such as Google, Facebook, and so on. They also send the big billing, $1,000 per hour or more. You'll get one of the senior partners when you have a billion-dollar valuation. But your little startup will get recent law school graduates.

Small firms charge less, but your work will be handled by the experienced lawyers. At small one-person or two-person law firms, they'll handle your case themselves.

You need a lawyer who works with startups. He or she should be familiar with the contracts for incorporation, stock allocation, investors, hiring, and intellectual property (IP) such as copyright, trademark, and patents. He should also know about tax issues.

An experienced lawyer also has connections to other lawyers, venture capital, investors, accountants, plus lots of founders. I know lawyers who handle over 120 startups.

You can't hire a lawyer who does medical insurance or whatever. They're not familiar with the startup world. Look for a lawyer who understands early-stage startups.

Almost all SV lawyers will talk with you for the first hour for free. Make sure the first consultation is free.

Often, you can pay legal bills with equity (stock). Or the lawyer may defer the billing, which means you can pay later when you have money. However, they'll also charge more. It may be better to pay a small bill now instead of a large bill later.

So how to find a lawyer? Like everything else in this book, talk with your connections. They'll recommend someone they like and trust.

➜ Be sure that you're billed for actual work. A lawyer invited one founder to coffee at the office. They chatted for an hour. He sent a bill for $400. That led to arguments.

Lawyers Outside of Silicon Valley

The main problem with non-SV lawyers is their lack of experience with startups and few or no connections to Silicon Valley. They'll also lead you to build a large company.

No matter where you're in the world, you can work with lawyers in Silicon Valley. They're comfortable with text messaging, email, and Skype. They get up early to talk with Europe and are up late to talk with China and India.

It's okay if you live in Germany, Spain, or China. You can do all of the legal paperwork by email and Skype. You can sign all of your documents via the web from your country. They can also help you with visa issues and how to deal with taxes if you're in France or South Korea.

You come to Silicon Valley, meet once or twice with your lawyer, and from then on, you meet by Skype or email.

➜ Several of the European founders told me they were amazed when they met with SV lawyers. European lawyers are stiff and formal. SV lawyers are casual and open.

Okay, So Do You Need to Incorporate?

So why do you incorporate? Traditionally, it was for liability. If you sell hot chocolate and someone buy a cup and pours it over her head, she can sue you (this is why the American legal system is so good: any idiot can sue for anything).

If you have a car, house, and dog and she wins, she'll get your car, house, and dog. Goodbye, ol' Rover, be a good dog. And bite her.

So you incorporate, which means you set up a legal structure that owns your hot chocolate company. All she can get is whatever the legal structure owns (a hot-chocolate delivery bicycle), but she can't get your house or dog. Incorporation protects your personal property from lawsuits.

However, this isn't really relevant for seed startups. If you're doing this in your home, then there won't be visitors who trip in the parking lot and break their nose, or pour hot chocolate over their heads. There's little risk of injury.

Startups have a different issue, namely, investors and buyers. Investors prefer to place their money in a corporation instead of your cookie jar. Buyers buy a corporation that owns the intellectual property. This means you incorporate for investors and buyers.

Don't rush to incorporate. You don't need to incorporate on the first day. Spend several months for customer interviews and development. When someone is ready to invest, you can incorporate in about five days.

You can start on handshake agreements. If you trust each other, that's fine. Many startups are based on handshakes for the first few months.

Maybe the best-known example is when Andy Bechtolsheim, co-founder of SUN, gave Larry Page and Sergey Brin a check for $100,000. They couldn't use it because they didn't have a business bank account or a corporation.

But if you don't really trust each other, then you should use a written agreement. The team may break up but some continue to develop the idea, or some may realize they can do it without you and they steal the idea. This has happened at quite a few startups, incl. Facebook and Twitter. Talk with a lawyer and get a basic agreement to protect your idea and IP (intellectual property).

How to Incorporate

If this is your first startup, you should work with a lawyer. It'll save you time and you can focus on the important stuff. After you've done this a few times, you can incorporate with online services such as Nolo or Clerky. Their website has lots of FAQs.

There are four kinds of corporations. The difference is how they're taxed:

- C-Corp: A C-corporation gets the income and pays the taxes, not the owners.

- S-Corp: In an S-corporation, the income passes through the corporation and goes to the owners, so the S-corp doesn't pay the taxes; the owners pay the taxes. That's why S-corps are called pass-through entities.

- LLC: Limited liability Company: This is an S-corp for partners. It also offers limited liability protection.

- PLLC: Professional limited liability company (PLLC): These are corporations for professional partnerships such as doctors and lawyers.

You can incorporate in any of the 50 US states: California, Alabama, whatever. However... most Silicon Valley companies incorporate in Delaware. The judges of the Delaware corporations court are leading experts in corporate law. Furthermore, Delaware corporate law is taught in most US law schools, so lawyers are familiar with Delaware law.

So you set up a Delaware C-corp. If you use another state, it may cause problems. Investors and buyers won't be familiar with that law. Which means they won't invest.

People make mistakes. Mark Zuckerberg incorporated Facebook in Florida because he didn't know any better.

It costs about $1,500 to $2,000 to incorporate with a lawyer. It's only $500 to incorporate online but I suggest you should work with a lawyer. You get the benefit of the lawyer's experience and network. SV lawyers often have 80-100 startups as clients, which gives them lots of connections to startups, boards, advisors, customers, M&A, IBs, and companies that may buy your startup. Talk with your advisors to find a lawyer.

When investors want to give you money or you sell the company, their lawyers want copies of the incorporation documents. You should make copies and keep them in two locations in case your house burns down.

You Hold a Board Meeting

You will be notified by Delaware when they approve your corporation. You then hold a board meeting with the directors. These are the people who make decisions for the corporation.

This is a minor legal technicality. Put yourself and two co-founders on the board. That's all.

In a way, a corporation is like a body in a coma. He lies there in a hospital bed and other people make decisions for him. That's what "corporation" means; it's legally a body that's managed by others, namely, the board of directors.

You decide who is on the board of the company. As the original founder, you're the chair of the board of directors. You add several more people. These can be your co-founders, senior advisors, or people whom you trust to help you to make decisions.

You should have an odd number on the board, such as three or five so there won't be a tie in a decision. More than five is too many.

Don't add friends or your cat to the board. Don't do stuff that you'll later have to undo because of investors or buyers.

You can hold your board meeting in person or via Skype.

You must keep minutes of the board meeting. This includes date, time, location, who is present, and what's said and decided.

Your lawyer can (and should) attend board meetings, but he shouldn't be a member of the board.

→ Make sure you have board members who'll vote with you, no matter what. We worked with a startup where Jenny started a company and built it up by hand for six months. Jenny brought in her best friend and with good intentions, split the company 50/50 with her friend. Six months later, it has grown nationwide so her best friend's husband, who was in enterprise corporate sales, joined the company. Jenny split the ownership 33/33/33. You can guess what happened. The best friend and husband held a board meeting and voted Jenny out of her company.

The Board Assigns the Officers of the Company

The board meeting also appoints the officers of the company. These are the people who do the day-to-day work of the company.

As chair of the board, you assign yourself to be the CEO. Others become the CTO, CFO, and so on. But these titles don't mean much in an early-stage startup.

The board and officers can be the same people or different people.

The Board Creates the Stock

The next agenda item for the board meeting is to issue the company's stock. This means they create stock. Just like an out-of-control copy machine, they can make new stock.

You decide how many shares your corporation will have. You can say it will be 1,000, one million, ten million, or ten billion shares. Or 342 shares. Any number you want. Generally, it's a million shares, but it's up to you.

You also set your stock's price. You can say the stock's price will be $0.01 (one cent), ten cents, one dollar, or whatever you like.

However, if you issue a million share at $0.01 per share, your startup's value is $10,000 (one million X $0.01 = $10,000) which means you have to pay taxes on that.

To reduce your taxes, you set the stock price at $0.0001 (three zeros). The value of the million shares is now $100 so the taxes will be low.

Your stock's $0.0001 price is the nominal value (which is also called the par value).

At this moment, the corporation owns its stock. The next item for your board meeting is to assign stock.

The Board Distributes the Stock

The board decides how much stock to give each person.

While writing this book, I talked with a bunch of startup founders and got different answers. The following is what seems to me to be a fair solution. You can change this to whatever you and your co-founders like.

Generally, startups use an 80/20 split. 80% of the stock goes to the founders and 20% goes to an options pool.

The founders share the 80% equally among themselves. Let's say there are three founders. You can make all sorts of splits, such as 55% to you; 20% to Laura; and 5% to Xiao Ping. But investors will ask, is Laura four times better than Xiao Ping? And won't Xiao Ping and Laura be unhappy that you get 55%? If your co-founders are important and everyone shares the work, you should split equally so each gets a third of the 80%, which is 26.66% for each.

The 20% options pool is stock that you'll give to advisors, staff, contractors, and others. For advisors, you may have several categories:

- Senior Advisors, who are actively involved in managing the startup. They may get 1-2%.
- Expert Advisors, who are generally experts on a topic (engineering, marketing, and so on). Give them 0.25% (a quarter of one share).
- Name advisors are well-known people who look good on your website. You can give them 0.1% in stock.

If you issue ten million shares, 1% is 100,000 shares, so 0.25% is 25,000 shares and 0.1% is 10,000 shares.

You can pay contractors in money or stock. At the beginning, you can lower your expenses by paying in stock. But this may lead you to overpay. If you give someone 10,000 shares to make a logo and you sell the company for $10m, the ten million shares are a dollar per share, so the logo may cost $10,000. You could have bought a logo for less than $100.

The contractor should consider the deferred fee as an investment in your company. If his bill is $5,000 and he accepts stock, then he's taking a substantial risk that he may not get paid, so he should expect a 10X return on his investment. This means he'll get $50,000. However, if the company fails, he may get nothing. As Yogi Berra said, it's easier to know the future after it happens.

Don't give stock to friends. It may sound nice to give a hundred shares to each follower in your Facebook page, but if you have more than 250 stock holders, you fall into a different SEC tax category. You may also have to pay a 40% gift tax.

Make sure your company's contract assigns any undistributed stock to back to the founders when there's an exit. Otherwise, the VCs will grab it for themselves.

➔ All co-founders should know how the stock has been distributed. If the founder keeps it secret that he gives 5% to one and 20% to another, eventually it will come out and that will cause problems.

➔ Similarly, co-founders (and everyone else, including advisors, staff, and contractors) should know how the amount of stock and the percentage of the company. It may sound good to get 1,000 shares, but if the company has ten million shares, that's 0.01%. You need to know the total and the percentage. You should get this in writing and keep the it in a safe place. Some companies have lied to their staff about this.

Restricted Stock and Options

There are two kinds of stock:

- Restricted Stock: When Rebecca joins the company as a co-founder, she gets restricted stock. It's called "restricted" because it has restrictions, such as vesting or it can't be transferred.
- Stock Options: When Olivia joins the company as an employee, she gets stock options.

Let's go through an example for each of these:

- Rebecca joins the startup as a co-founder. To make it easy, let's say she gets 10%. The company has ten million shares, so she will get one million restricted shares.
- Rebecca gets her stock at the nominal value, which is also called the par value. You can say she gets her stock at par.
- The nominal value is $0.0001 per share, which is $100 (one million shares X $0.0001 per share = $100). She gives the company a check for $100 and the company gives her one million shares.
- However, her stocks are restricted, which means there are conditions, such as vesting. If she violates the conditions, she loses her stocks.

- As the co-founders give checks to your corporation, the stock gains real value.

This can be a good deal for Rebecca. If the startup is sold for ten million, the shares go up to $1 per share. She paid $0.0001 to buy a share that became $1. Her $100 becomes $1m. That's her bonus for joining early.

What about stock for employees and advisors?

- Olivia joins the startup as a staff employee. She gets an option to buy 10,000 shares of stock. The company has ten million shares so her 10,000 shares is 0.01% of the company.

- On the day she joins, the company stock's value is $0.25, so her strike price is $0.25. As the company gets more investors and revenue goes up, the valuation increases. Olivia's options increase in value. Her shares go up from $0.25 to $2 per share. Her stock is now worth $20,000.

- But Olivia has options to buy the stock, which means she doesn't yet own it. By "exercising her options", she buys her stock. She pays $0.25 for stock that is worth $2.00. If she exercises all of her options, she pays $500 and gets $20,000 in stock.

Both restricted stock and stock options use a vesting schedule. This means you get part of your stock at the end of the month or quarter.

Why Startups Use Vesting

Whether it's restricted stock for co-founders or stock options for staff and advisors, you get your stock on a vesting schedule. Let's see what that means.

Startups use vesting to make sure the team keeps working. If a startup gives Olivia 100% of her shares on the first day, she'll quickly realize she doesn't have to do any more work. This is the same as if you hire a staffer and give him 100% of his annual salary on the first day. Good luck on him showing up on the second day!

That's why everyone in the company, both founders, team, and advisors, is on a vesting schedule.

For example, a four-year vesting schedule can be 25% on a one-year cliff with vesting of the remainder on a monthly or quarterly schedule. Let's see what that means.

Vesting schedules can be one year, two years, four years, or more. Generally, it's four years in Silicon Valley. All other models are possible, such as one-year schedule and so on, but no investor will agree to those. They want a four-year schedule because they want to tie you to the company for four years.

Vesting calendars can be monthly or quarterly. In the following example, we'll use a monthly calendar.

Rebecca is a co-founder with restricted stock. Her vesting schedule is 25% with a one-year cliff with the remainder of the stock over the next three years, so this covers four years. Let's say she joins the company as a co-founder on the first of September, 2016, so her vesting day is a full calendar year later on the second of September 2017. When she joined the company, she paid for her stock so she owns it already. On September 2, 2017, she gets 25% of her stock.

If the startup uses a monthly vesting calendar, then on the last day of each month after her vesting day, she gets more of her stock. Twelve months multiplied by three years is 36 months, so every month, she gets $1/36^{th}$ of her remaining stock. 750,000 shares divided by 36 months is 20,833 shares per month.

Olivia is a staff employee with stock options. Her vesting schedule is also 25% with a one-year cliff with the remainder over the next three years. She joins the company as a staff worker on the first of September, 2016, so her vesting day is a full calendar year later on the second of September 2017. On that day, she can exercise the option (use her rights) to buy 25% of her stock at her strike price or she can just leave them there until later. She gives the company accountant a check for $625 and gets a receipt for her 2,500 shares. She can hold the stock or she can ask the company's stockbroker to sell them for her.

On the last day of each month after her vesting day, she has the option to buy more of the remaining 75% of her stock. Twelve months multiplied by three years is 36 months, so each month, she can buy $1/36^{th}$ of her stock. 7,500 shares divided by 36 months is 208 shares per month.

Olivia can pay each month. She can also leave after four years and have additional time to exercise her options (buy her stock). Some companies give her 90 days; others may give her several years. The longer, the better for her because she'll have time to think about it.

Olivia's options have an expiration date. If there's a five-year expiration, then she must buy her stock within five years after she's fully vested or she loses the right to buy her options.

A few years later, Emily joins the company as a staffer and get 1,000 shares at a $10 strike price. The stock goes up to $20. If she buys her stock, she would have to pay $100,000 (10,000 shares X $10 strike price) but she doesn't have that money. No problem. Her company's stock broker first sells her shares for $200,000, then deducts her $100,000, and gives her the remaining $100,000 (minus taxes). This lets her exercise her options without cash upfront.

The 83B Election

As the startup grows, valuation goes up so your founder shares become more valuable. You're getting richer, which means you must pay taxes. But you haven't yet sold the company so you're rich in theory but have no money to pay taxes.

If your startup is in the US, you can avoid taxes by filing an 83B election. This is a letter that you send to the IRS within 30 days of getting your stock. Use a proof-of-mailing to prove that you did this. Your lawyer will help you with this.

If your startup is another country, you'll have to check with your country's tax laws. Talk with a tax attorney who has experience with startups and taxes.

What about Salaries for Founders?

At first, there's no money, so no salaries. When you get investors, the co-founders can get a bit of salaries. This is generally low. The goal is the exit, where you can make millions of dollars.

Why do founders get such big rewards? Because they take a big risk. They work very hard for several years and get nothing. They also do creative and innovative work yet get nothing. They're not just staffers.

Single-Trigger and Double-Trigger

A trigger is an event that starts a legal clause. For example, if the company is sold, then Laura's vesting schedule is accelerated and she vests 100% at once. Trigger events can be the sale of a company, an IPO, or she leaves the company, either involuntary (fired) or voluntary (quits).

If the event is the sale of the company, then that's a single-trigger acceleration. This rewards her for her contribution to the success.

However, the buyer may buy the company and get rid of people they don't want. That's two triggers (buy and fire) so you use double-trigger acceleration. The company is sold and she's fired within a time frame, perhaps 9-24 months after closing. If she's fired within that period after the sale, she gets her stock. This protects her from the VCs.

There may also be a pre-closing window (such as three to six months before the sale) to block preemptive firing. A company knows it will be sold, so the VCs fire people early to take away their stock. That stock of course goes to the VCs.

These triggers should cover both the co-founders and advisors. When you add staff, they should also be covered by double-triggers.

What Can Go Wrong

Many things can go wrong. Key people quit, you misunderstand the customers, the startup doesn't deliver, a competitor develops a better product, investors won't give you more money, the economy crashes, or a giant sea monster eats your office in San Francisco. The company fails and the stock has zero value.

Patents, Copyright, and Trademarks

Your intellectual property (IP) includes patents, copyrights, trademarks, and so on.

In the beginning, you'll pivot several times or even quit the idea, so it's better to wait until baby can walk.

When you have an idea, you can file for a provisional patent. That's like a temporary holder on your idea. The fee starts at about $65 and it's easy to file. You then have a year to decide whether to file for a patent.

Your lawyer can help you with this or put you in touch with a patent lawyer.

A US patent is about $5,000. Some lawyers however may charge far more. Don't pay that.

You may have to consider patents in other countries. Your lawyer can recommend a foreign patent lawyer.

Legal Documents and Contracts

Contracts with phrases such as *the party of the first part* are pretentious. If you can't understand it, send it back and ask for it in plain English. Luckily, young lawyers also prefer clear language.

You can get free copies of legal contracts at websites such as LegalZoom, Nolo, and Clerky.

Finally, a contract isn't really worth much. Any lawyer will tell you a 100-page contract is worthless if the other guy wants to cheat you. If you don't trust the other guy, don't do business with him.

Summary

You have to understand the legal stuff enough that you don't make mistakes. The best solution is to get an experienced lawyer who is on your side. Talk with founders who have done several startups to find a lawyer.

7: Funding Stuff

Let's look now at investors and funding. This means the money.

This is one of the longest chapters in this book because it covers something that people don't want to talk about. Money is one of the central issues in modern society but it's also taboo to talk about it. Funding is an important part of Silicon Valley, yet people know very little about venture capital, VCs, where they get their money, and how they work. Let's look at the implications of funding for your startup.

First, Do You Really Need Money?

Many people assume your startup has to raise money. There are benefits to funding:

- Funding lets you grow faster. You could spend several years to grow slowly or get a vitamin boost and grow fast.
- You can pay your bills, pay the rent, and buy some food.
- Validation. If someone invests in your startup, others will think your startup is a good idea. In a way, yes, it's validation, but in a deeper sense, it's not validation. VCs invest in lots of companies for many reasons (it's a good project, they're placing bets on many projects, they don't know what they're doing, and so on). Your true validation comes when customers buy your product.
- Experience and connections: The investor wants your company to grow, so she'll share her connections and experience with you.

Funding also brings problems:

- It's the investors' money and they want to keep an eye on it, so they will supervise you. They'll set timetables and deadlines.
- You have five investors? You have five bosses. They'll tell you what to do. Some investors will insist that you hire their lazy nephew.

- Investors want growth so they'll push for sales, which means you'll have to develop marketing and sales strategies, hire marketing and sales staff, manage campaigns, get an office, and so on. All of this takes attention away from development.
- The more money you raise, the less of your startup that you will own, so you'll get less when you sell.
- When you have too much money, you solve problems by throwing money at it. Many startups do this until they run out of money.

If you don't need investor money, don't take it.

Small startups must solve problems. If they don't have money, they become creative. When Google was just a few people and no money, they had to build their servers. They bought cheap computers and used Linux, which is free.

After you build the first successful startup and walk away with a bit of money, you can fund your own projects.

→ Several founders built their company without any funding. This meant they weren't under pressure from investors for growth and revenue.

Little Bird Funding: Cheep, Cheep!

You're researching your idea in the first few months of your startup. This means you don't have anything to show investors (so you won't get money) and you don't have anything to sell (so you won't get money).

Which means you should be as cheap as possible. Every dollar you save is less equity that you give away. Spend as little as possible.

- If you're young, you can live at home with your parents. If you have a partner or spouse, he or she can support you for a while.
- Use free software. Microsoft and Google will give you pretty much everything for free.
- Don't incorporate or hire lawyers or accountants. Do that later when you have money. You can write a short agreement among your team for now.
- Paying bills with stock sounds good, but you're overpaying. Instead of $100 today, you'll pay $1,000 tomorrow. Pay today as little as possible.

- If there are expenses before you incorporate, these are loans to the company. Everyone should keep receipts for travel, food, supplies, costs, and so on. After you get funding, you can be reimbursed.

Interview your customers. Develop your idea. Work with your advisors. If you can show a viable business model, then you can get funding and move to the next step.

➔ Spend as little as possible. The more cash you have, the more options you'll have, a longer runway, and more pivots. Because you won't be desperate for money, you'll be able to get better terms.

➔ Several years ago, a number of investors used millions of dollars to fund startups in India. Because they had money, they built traditional startups with large infrastructure, lots of staff, and focused on growth and revenues. A few years later, these were gone. In India and similar markets, you have to start small, discover what works, and survive the mistakes to build sustainable companies.

➔ Many of the founders are in their early 20s and returned home after college. This is a very good way to lower expenses in the early stage. You also have a strong advantage against competitors. It can cost $3-5,000 per month just to have office space.

➔ Several founders had family who had office buildings so they were able to set up offices there. This lets them keep costs down.

Investment or Loan?

People often ask me if you have to pay back the investment.

If you borrow money from a bank, you repay the loan and interest. If you borrow $100,000 at 10% annual interest, then you pay back $100,000 (the loan) and $10,000 (the interest) a year later.

An investment is a bet that your project will succeed. If your project fails, you don't pay it back. The investor knows she may lose the money.

The investor is taking a risk (the money may be lost) so she asks for a large payback.

If the investment is successful, you pay back the investment plus a multiple, such as 5X or 10X. If the multiple is 5X, then you pay back $100,000 plus five times the amount ($500,000).

Some investors have gotten 30,000X return. No other business offers that (okay, legally). That's why people with money everywhere in the world are interested in Silicon Valley.

What happens if you lose the money? If you did a lousy job and wasted the money, the investors may cry a lot, never talk with you again, and warn their friends. If you did a good job and tried hard but it didn't work out, they'll understand and many of them will invest in your next project.

Only a few projects are successful. Many people say "failure isn't an option," but in Silicon Valley, failure is likely. When it works, it pays very well, so people keep trying.

Make sure your investors understand it's risky and you'll do the best you can.

What If You're Not in Silicon Valley?

Investors in Europe, South America, China, and the US East Coast (NYC, Chicago, and so on) are conservative and avoid risks. They want to see a product, users, sales, and revenue before they invest. It's safer for them but they'll get fewer opportunities. They tend to look at the current reality, not the potential.

➔ In many countries, there's a general lack of experience and knowledge about investing in startups. They prefer to invest in things they know and understand, such as property. If they invest, the amounts will be low.

➔ Several European founders told me a Swedish investor won't invest in a Swedish startup in Stockholm, but if the Swedish startup sets up an office in Palo Alto, it's now a Silicon Valley startup so he'll invest in that. European and Chinese investors want to invest in Silicon Valley, so money from Asia, Europe, and South America comes to Silicon Valley.

➔ Another problem with investors outside of Silicon Valley is their attitude against youth. In several countries, investors will insist the founder team of 21-year olds accept a "adult" co-founder in the team. That'll kill the party.

All in all, it's easier to raise money in Silicon Valley because there are more investors and they have experience with startups.

What Are the Chances?

Here are the general numbers at a typical VC firm:

- 4,000 proposals are reviewed yearly
- 400 startups get a 30-minute phone call to discuss the project
- 100 are invited to a one-hour meeting
- 20 get funded

About 15 SV startups produce 95% of all returns in Silicon Valley.

It's very hard to know the real numbers but it's somewhere in this range. In an average work day, VC staffers review perhaps twenty proposals, do five phone screening calls, and hold two meetings.

Types of Funding

There are many ways to fund your startup. Here are some ideas:

- Self-funded. You and your team share the expenses. You have day jobs, you do side projects, or you live on your savings or credit cards.
- Some of the founders had existing first or second startups that are producing revenue so they live from that.
- Unemployment Money: Some cities offer money for unemployed who want to start a business. One of the founders used this to get started.
- Revenue: Some startups start making money very early so they can live on their own revenue.
- Friends and family: Spouse, partner, parents, extended family, friends, alumni, church, social clubs, co-workers, or advisors fund the project.
- Crowd funding: People donate money for interesting projects. There's Kickstarter, Indiegogo, and many other crowd-funding sites. One founder used this. You need strong social marketing for it to work so this is a case where you'll need to do marketing while building your early-stage startup.
- Startup contests: Companies and governments hold startup contests. Many of these offer substantial prizes. I've met founders who got $50,000 or $100,000.
- Accelerators: Some accelerators give you money. Y-Combinator gives $130,000 to each startup.

- Government grants: Many city, state, and national governments invest in startups to create jobs (which also produce taxes).
- Universities: A number of universities are funding their students' startups. There are also investment groups for alumni of Stanford, Berkeley, MIT, Yale, Harvard, and other schools.
- Corporate investment: Large companies invest in startups in their field with the hope of finding projects to acquire.
- Angels: These are people who made money in (for example) biotech so they're willing to invest in biotech because they know the field.
- Venture Capital. VCs raise money from large investors (insurance companies, large companies, family foundations, government, endowments, universities, and so on) and invest the money in startups.

If your startup made a good return for your investors, you can easily get funding for your next startup from the same investors. One fellow sold his startup and with only an idea, he raised $2m for his next startup.

➜ One of the founders is on his third (or fourth?) startup. He doesn't need investor money. With the connections that he has built along the way, he'll get friends at large companies to buy the startup.

➜ If you're building a non-profit startup, then it's unlikely that you'll get investors. However, you can get donors to contribute. Another possibility is crowd funding.

➜ Another idea is to get funding via Angel List (angel.co). Look for $5-10K investments which means you get lots of investors and their advice and connections. Startups with lots of angels find it easy to get more angels because the angels tell other angels.

➜ University and government grants sometimes create a problem. For some fields and in some countries, there are plenty of grants so startups go from grant to grant and never launch. They need to face reality. Some need to die. This is like university graduate students who get graduate degrees, one after the other, so they don't have to work.

By the way, angels were wealthy people who sponsored theatrical plays on Broadway in New York City in the early 1900s.

About VC Firms

A VC firm has five to ten general partners (GPs) and principals who look for deals and handle due diligence. There are also associates, junior associates, analysts, and interns.

There are about 800 VC firms in the US but only about 400 are active. About 100 are in Silicon Valley. Most of the money goes to Silicon Valley VCs. You can learn more at the National Venture Capital Group (NVCA).

Many VC firms are on Sand Hill Road, which is a long street from Palo Alto to the 280 freeway, lined with low office buildings. You can often see the VCs behind the buildings, rolling down the hills of cash.

Each VC handles about 4-6 startups, depending on the stage of the ten-year fund. When the fund is new, he's working with many startups. As the fund gets older (and some of the startups shut down), he'll spend more time with a few startups to prepare them for the exit. VCs also deal with LPs (their investors), other co-investors, co-founders, customers, and so on. They also meet with the media to promote the startups.

VCs are ranked by their return on investment. The more they make, the higher their ranking. There are rankings for VC firms and GPs. A low-ranked VC firm is often willing to invest because it's desperate or crazy.

In the last ten years, VC funds have gotten larger so their investments have also grown. VCs moved up from seed startups to late-stage startups. In response, angels and accelerators stepped in to fund seed startups. A new class of micro-VCs appeared. There are about 225 micro-VCs (and about half are in SV) who make $25K-$500K investments.

➔ Don't worry about the VC's ranking. It's up to you to use the funding to build your startups.

➔ VCs don't solve your startup's problems. You have to figure out your problems and solve them yourself. What you get from VCs is money to accelerate your startup.

How to Meet Investors

There are two ways of meeting investors: cold calls and warm calls.

- A cold call is when you call someone you don't know. There's no connection between you and him.

- A warm call is when you're introduced to someone through a mutual friend. He tells the other person that he knows you and trusts you. The other person will then talk with you as a favor to his friend.

Your goal is to get a first meeting. If there's interest on both sides, then you have follow-up meetings.

Remember what Reid Hoffman said about connections? That he only talks with people who have connections to him? Many VCs and angels look at proposals only if these come from trusted friends.

Talk with your friends, family, and co-workers to find people who know other people. When you talk with potential co-founders and advisors, ask about their connections.

➜ You're going to do a lot of meetings. In general, you'll do 100 meetings (five meetings daily) for each $100,000 in funding. You'll become very good at quickly saying what you're doing.

➜ If you have a good team and a good idea, people will tell other people. Advisors, heads of the top incubators, and professors at the business schools are constantly asked by investors and VCs about new startups.

➜ Silicon Valley VCs say startups shouldn't send unsolicited proposals because they ignore those. But in other countries, VCs have less to do, so this may work. One of the founders did that. He sent proposals to 35 VC firms in his country. He got 16 meetings. Three said yes and two finally invested around $1.5m. It took nine months. Try it in your country.

➜ One investor used his online social networks to let people know what he was doing and investors contacted him through that.

➜ But a meeting with an investor may mean anything. Some investors are interested in a market, so they'll meet with startups in that market to see what they can learn.

➜ And there's the friend-of-a-friend-of-a-friend. One founder's brother told a friend, who told another friend, who knew someone who collected cars. He invested. You should have a good grandmother pitch that makes it easy for people to tell other people what you're doing.

There are people who call themselves VCs and offer $1m in funding if you pay a small $15,000 setup fee. They're fake VCs.

What's a Pitch?

The word *pitch* comes from baseball when the pitcher throws the ball to the batter. You pitch when you show your proposal to an investor.

A pitch event is a conference where five or ten startups pitch to an audience of investors. There are daily pitch events in Silicon Valley.

A jury of three or six VCs and investors sit at the front of the room. Generally, you talk for two minutes, followed by three minutes for questions and answers from them. Or it's three minutes for pitch and three minutes for questions. Or it's thirty minutes.

There may be a small $20-50 fee to cover costs and food, but don't pay $500 or whatever.

Go to as many pitch events as you can. See what they ask. After the event is over, you can talk with the investors and tell them about your project.

→ One founder with many years of experience in Silicon Valley said pitch events are entertainment. He didn't think it was a place for serious investment consideration. He said first-time founders should go to these to get experience in pitching and improve the pitch deck. Don't expect to get funding and don't feel disappointed if you don't get funding offers.

→ The quality of investors depends on the quality of the event. Top events get top investors. You should pitch anyway for the experience. You should also pitch as often as you can. You get more confidence.

About Your Pitch Deck

Here are a bunch of ideas about pitch decks:

- Use a ten-page pitch deck. Don't go beyond twelve pages. If you can do it in three slides, that's better. I've seen people try to present 60-page decks and they get cut off before they get to the good part.
- Each slide should have a single idea and not more than three bullet points on a page. The bullet points should be short.
- The pitch deck should be a Powerpoint that opens in both Windows and Apple devices.

- Ask someone with good writing skills to review your pitch. Your deck should appear professional. Headings, fonts, colors, and format should be consistent. Spelling, grammar, capitalization should be correct.
- Use page numbers in the slides so you can refer to a slide.
- Don't read your slides to the audience. Talk about your slides.

Keep a copy of your deck on a flash drive on your keychain, on your phone, and in your cloud folder so you always have it.

The Pitch Deck, Page by Page

Key Idea: Let's look at each page of your pitch deck:

- Slide 1: The Title Page. Your company name, logo, a one-line description of what your company does, the date (such as May 2017), and the audience.
- Slide 2: The Founder Team. Name, title, university degree, experience, expertise, and professional photos. You could include your advisors.
- Slide 3: The Market Opportunity: How big is the market opportunity (in US$) by country, state, or city. For example, $1B in US, $300m in California, or $25m in Palo Alto.
- Slide 4: State the Problem: How does it affect your users? What does the problem cost the user in time or money?
- Slide 5: The Product: How will your product, technology, or service solve the problem. Include photos or screen shots.
- Slide 6: Competitors: Who are the major players in this market? How is your product better than the competitors?
- Slide 7: The Business Model: How your business will make money.
- Slide 8: Financial Overview: A simple 5-year financial projection.
- Slide 9: The Ask: How much money have you raised so far? Who has invested? How much money do you need? Ask for the money.
- Slide 10: Your Contact Information: Name, email, cell phone, website, and postal mailing address.

You could skip slides seven and eight. Just say the money stuff will be solved later.

You can download a sample pitch deck at the webpage for this book. Get that, edit, and start pitching.

→ There's lot of discussion about the ask (slide #9). Some say you should ask for the money. Others say you should not ask for money. They say if the investors are interested, you should have several meetings and then ask for money. Whether you ask for money or not, it depends on your industry, country, and so on. Ask your advisors about this.

The Pitch

When you pitch, you're showing investors how they'll make money with you. Show that you have assembled a team that can do the work and solve problems. Show that you've interviewed customers, identified a problem, and have a solution.

The pitch is a business offer, not a job interview. Your startup's CEO should pitch. Investors are looking at the idea but they're also looking at whether you have the leadership and confidence to lead the project.

Discuss your idea with your team and advisors until you're totally clear on every issue. Be sure that you understand funding concepts such as convertible notes and dilution. Otherwise, investors will realize you're unprepared.

People will ask questions that you can't answer. Write down the question, tell them that you'll look into it, and send a follow-up email within 24 hours.

→ For example, an investor once asked the weight of a cubic foot of snow. That depends on humidity, so you should also know the range (between 20 pounds to 60 pounds) (and figure this out in cubic feet, cubic meters, pounds, kilos, Fahrenheit, and centigrade).

→ Don't go by yourself. Have a co-founder with you to take notes. Write down every objection and figure out answers. If you can, video the event.

→ Go to pitch events and see how others pitch. You'll see there is wide difference between good and bad pitches. For one startup's pitch, we practiced fifteen times. Get a pitch coach if you can.

→ Ask your advisors and professors if they can suggest pitch events.

Meetings

When investors meet you, they're evaluating if you have the ability to lead a startup. Show enthusiasm and confidence. Have a firm handshake and make eye contact. Be ready to talk about your project.

Research the person and company before the meeting. Know who they are, what they can do for you, what you want from them, and what you can do for them.

Be ready to say which metrics (such as sales funnel, revenues, subscriptions, and so on) are important for your project and how you will collect those numbers.

Be careful with metrics such as registrations, users, likes, social mentions, and so on. Those don't matter much and are easy to fake.

How Investors Evaluate You in Pitch Events

There are several ways for the judges and investors at pitch events to judge you.

Sometimes, the investors and judges use a form to score you. That form covers the following issues:

- **The Market Opportunity:** What's the size of the market? What's the TAM (total addressable market)? What's the business model? What's the potential investment ROI? What's the likely exit?

- **The Technology:** What's your technology? What's the IP advantage? What's the differentiation from top competitors?

- **The Team:** Your team's qualifications, knowledge, experience, and track record. Can you do the project? Can you solve the problems that come up?

- **Presentation Ability:** Do you appear confident, knowledgeable, and professional? Will you be able to lead a team, talk with investors, and sell to clients?

You can edit your pitch deck to cover those points.

Other times, the judges don't have a form. They ask questions based on their experience and interests. You should go to as many pitch events as possible and see what kind of questions they ask.

➜ Founders agreed it's intense to pitch. One founder team was pitching as much as seven times a day with only two hours of sleep and they had a lot of fun because they were successfully raising money for their startup. If you're excited about your startup, the investors feel the excitement and want to join.

➜ However, pitch events can also be frustrating if investors aren't paying attention, they're looking at their phones, or don't look at you.

➜ If an investor is a financial person or an engineer, he'll often only look at the metrics. If you've researched an issue and state a number, he'll challenge you by asking for the source. When you put numbers in your presentation, be ready to show authoritative sources.

Always Be Ready to Pitch

It's 7 a.m., you're in line at Starbucks for your daily decaf skinny iced caramel upside-down macchiato with extra kiddie sprinkles on top and the woman standing next to you in REI fleece and sweatpants asks, "What are you doing?"

She may be a VC who is looking for startups. Or she may be wondering why you're ordering such a crazy thing.

Always be ready to say, "We're doing medical records" or, "I'm ordering this for my six-year old daughter."

Be ready to do a 30-minute presentation in two minutes. Be ready to pitch without your slides.

➜ At a pitch event, the projector burned out. Only a few could do their pitches without slides.

➜ At a pitch event, one of the startups doesn't show up. The VC asked if anyone in the audience wanted to pitch.

➜ Two guys from a Korean startup are in San Francisco to look for clients and investors. They're in line at burger place. They start talking with the woman next to them. She realizes the tool is something that I could use for a client. She text messages me. I ask if they can be in Palo Alto in 45 minutes. They show up at the office. I pick them up in the lobby and walk them into an ongoing meeting of twelve people. I say, "Go ahead and show us what you have." After thirty minutes, we say, "Okay, when can we start using it?"

Crazy Questions

Sometimes, it's obvious they never looked at your material. Or they interrupt to ask something else. Or questions are irrelevant or a bit crazy. One guy asked, "Have you considered a Java API and if not, why not?" Some investors are aggressive and you wonder if he's testing your confidence or just being arrogant. And sometimes, clueless investors may ridicule your idea.

Some investors will look at how you present. Some investors like to ask hard questions in a chaotic way or confront you to see how you react; others do this because they don't really know what to ask.

Okay, here's reality: investors often don't prepare for your meetings. You work on your beautiful Powerpoint for 72 hours non-stop, send it, show up at the meeting, and he says, "So what is it that your company does?"

When They Say Yes

There are several reasons they say yes:

- Graham and Dodd Investors: Two professors at Columbia business school developed criteria for rational investing based on metrics and value. Investors who make decisions like this are called Graham and Dodd investors.
- Wise investing: The VCs invest, based on their experience and wisdom. Also called a wild guess.
- Strategic investing: The VCs invest in a project because it helps them with another project or they want to block a competitor.
- Herd investing: They invest because that's where the herd is stampeding. This is also FOMO investing.

It can take six to nine months of meetings to get to yes. Often, you'll have to teach the investor about the business opportunity.

➜ One founder said he openly shared information about the product, market, and data with investors because he felt that investors could tell if you were hiding something. He also wanted investors who were open with him. Most of the founders said they were open with their investors.

➜ Several founders said they had developed elaborate financial spreadsheets for their first startup, but investors didn't look at them and everything was constantly changing, so the spreadsheets were useless.

When They Say No

There are several reasons they say no:

- You didn't make it clear that you have the team, found a problem to solve, or it will make money. Review the video of your presentation and watch their faces to see if you can find where they didn't understand you.
- He's not interested, wants to do something else, or it doesn't fit in his field or strategy.
- The investor is just looking. He's learning about the market, he may not be ready to invest, or just likes the attention.

If you think VCs are hard on you, they're just having fun. VCs get flattened when they go to their institutional investors.

As I wrote earlier, just as an investment isn't validation of your project, rejection doesn't mean your idea is bad. The real test is whether your customers use your product.

Pandora was rejected by 88 investors. It's worth $3B today. Menlo Ventures turned down Facebook. OVP Venture Partners turned down Amazon. Warren Buffet said no to Intel. Venrock rejected Xerox, Tanden, and Compaq. ARCH Venture Partners rejected Netscape and Canaan Partners rejected Juniper. Kleiner-Perkins declined VMWare. Tim Draper turned down Google and Facebook. Nolan Bushnell turned down 33% of Apple for $50,000 (which would be $400B today).

When to Raise Money

Most startups start looking for money on the first day. They're looking for someone to cover the costs of building the business. They're also looking for someone to pay for their food and rent.

This causes two problems. First, it's very difficult to raise money if you don't yet have a viable business. You should be developing your product.

The second problem is worse. Let's say you get money. The investor wants a return on his money, so you suddenly have a boss who says stop wasting time on customer interviews and start making money. Your team will turn into a sales and marketing operation with a weak product. Every week, you must report on how much money you made and how you'll increase that. You go to market with a weak product and your startup will fail.

If you first discover the customers' problems and create a solution, you'll have a business model and it'll be much easier to raise money.

The Ask: How Much to Raise

So how much money do you ask for? Talk with your advisors, guess your runway, estimate the costs, add a safety cushion, and round it up.

You'll notice that I didn't say "calculate"; I said "guess." You could do a spreadsheet and add up every number, but reality will be different. What's your runway when you'll likely pivot four or five times in the next six months?

➜ Don't overdo it. A friend told me about his project. It was fairly easy to build and he only needed $200,000. He said he was going to raise $100m. Investors aren't idiots (well, not all of them). They've heard thousands of proposals and have a good sense of what it takes. They'll think he hasn't any idea of what he's doing. Again, come up with a number and discuss it with your advisors.

You shouldn't raise too much money. It's a lot of work to raise money that you won't need. Worse than that, investors will also get a greater share of your company. Raise just what you need and give away as little as possible.

➜ How much? If you only need $200,000 and you ask for that, nobody will take you seriously. That's very small. Ask for $500,000. At one of our startups, we estimated that we needed $250,000 so we raised $500,000 and kept the extra for safety. Later, we returned the extra money to investors.

You may be wondering about *the ask*. This is a new word for a request, as in, "what's the ask?" Yes, it's a bit odd, but people say it.

Your Runway

That last section brings up the runway. Okay, an airplane needs about 13,000 feet (2.5 miles or 4,000m) of runway to take off.

Let's say your seed startup will need twelve months to take off and start making money. So your runway is twelve months.

You don't want to get to the end and then find that you need more money. Figure your runway, the monthly costs (rent, pizza, and so on), and whatever else, add a bit more, and go with that. Raise enough money to get you to the end of the runway.

Checks, Convertible Notes, SAFE, or Cash?

Besides checks, there are several other types of funding:

- Convertible notes: Instead of a loan, you use a convertible note. The investor loans money to the startup. When the note is due (for example, in a year), the investor gets equity (stock), not interest.

- YC's SAFE: Y-Combinator developed the SAFE (Simple Agreement for Future Equity) to replace the convertible note. The SAFE is a way to give money without creating debt. Learn more at ycombinator.com/documents/#safe

- Cash: An investor said okay, she'll invest $50,000. Cash. She had it in a paper bag. We counted it, gave her a receipt, and four of us walked to the bank.

Talk with your lawyers and advisors.

Problems with Investors

Your interests and the investor's interests are not the same. An investor will invest in 30 or 40 companies but most of these will fail. When he sees that a company is failing, he'll pull out so he can put his time and money in the ones that look better. Which means if you're not doing well, he'll quit on you. You have only one life to live, but he has 30 lives.

Some VCs don't know what they're talking about, but insist they're right, so you get endless arguments.

The VCs also fight among themselves. I won't go into this but when that happens, guess who loses?

➔ Some founders said investors often didn't explain why they said no or why they didn't like the idea.

Due Diligence on You

Before VCs decide to invest in you, they carry out *due diligence* (DD). This means they research your background.

They hire DD companies to check your credit history, graduation and degree, work history, past addresses, criminal history, and so on. They'll also contact your co-founders, advisors, and other people to ask about your background, technical skill, work style, personality, connections, and future plans. They ask your co-founder how well he knows you.

The level of due diligence can range from a FBI-level background check to a "yeah, whatever." Some hire DD companies, some look at your Facebook page, and others go with the lead investor's opinion.

➔ A number of founders said the investors and due diligence focused on the business plan and personal chemistry but ignored the technical issues. Several said the investors didn't look at even one line of code.

➔ Some VCs understand metrics and will ask in depth about this. But if your startup is growing fast and the VC ask many questions which takes too much time to answer, you can push back or go with another investor.

The result is a 10-20 page due dili report on you.

Due Diligence on Your VCs

You do due dili too (you knew that was coming, right?) on your investors. In a game where people can earn billions, there's strong incentive to lie. Review your investor's website, blog, Twitter, Facebook, and LinkedIn. You should also research him in CrunchBase and Angel.co. If he says he graduated from Harvard, see if he really went to Harvard.

You can hire the same DD companies to research the VCs. It's about $3,000 for DD on a VC. You'll find out about his side deals, conflicts of interests, arrests for fraud, his lifetime ban from Wall Street, his wife, mistress, and girlfriend.

When you begin talking with investors, ask your connections. Talk with your advisors. Check your forums for founders.

➔ Founders should do due diligence on their large investors. Founders should ask how the investor works with startups. You should talk with startups where he has invested. Ask if he is helpful or annoying, what value does he add, what connections does he have, and what kind of advice does he offer. Founders end up with the wrong kind of investors if they're desperate for funding and take whatever they can get without checking.

➔ You should also carry out due diligence when you're selling the startup. This includes the M&A person who is handling the sale (look for conflict of interest or problems with fraud) and the buyer (make sure they have the ability to pay). Don't spend months in a sales negotiation only to find there are problems that prevent a sale.

The Business Models

You'll be asked about the business model. This means how you plan to make money. There are several ways:

- Ad revenue: You place ads on your site and make money when people click. Media sites and many apps do this.
- Affiliate: You offer stuff from other companies and when someone buys, you get a percentage.
- Subscriptions: People pay for monthly or annual subscriptions. This works for magazines, newspapers, and software.
- Sales: You sell your product.

Or just tell them you're a Zen Buddhist and you don't care about money. That's probably a better answer because at this point, you're still figuring out if there's a business. Later, when you begin to sell your products, you can try various business models.

Your Advantage over the VCs

Thousands of investors and VCs have the same thing: too much money. And they all want the same thing. More money.

However, you have the ability to put together a competent team and figure out good ideas.

This gives you the advantage. They need you, but you can always go to another investor. I should underline that in bold italics. There are many of them but only a few of you.

What VCs Really Want

The best way to deal with VCs is to understand what they really need. VCs set up funds that have a ten-year life cycle. They invest in startups during the first six years. Since most startups fail, they need about 20-24 startups which means they must add a startup every quarter for six years.

A new fund is on the hunt for deals. VCs invest in what they know. If you're doing biotech, don't bother with fintech investors. If you match their industry profile (biotech, AI, whatever) and you have a good team, you solve their problem and they'll invest.

At the beginning of a fund's cycle, VCs have lots of money so they're likely to make decisions on macho emotions. After a few years, they only need a few more deals so they start to evaluate carefully. Look at the VC's fund history. If it's just starting, you have a chance.

How VCs Make Money

It also helps to understand how VCs make money.

- A VC announces he will create a new $100m fund.
- It will be a ten-year fund. If he sets it up in 2017, he'll manage the fund for ten years and the payout will be in 2027.
- He names it with a Roman numeral, for example Fund IV, or he names it after his Rottweiler or a Star Trek villain.
- He raises the money for the fund. He goes around to his frat buddies or Harvard, Stanford, or Wharton business school alumni who manage money at large mutual funds, pension funds, university endowments, sovereign wealth funds (such as Norway or Saudi Arabia), family offices, charities, and other groups with billions of dollars.
- Because of tax laws, the VC has to put some of his money into the fund, so he puts in 1%, which is $1m in this case.
- The VC gets 2-and-20. That means 2% and 20%. The 2% is the management fee, so for his $100m fund, he gets $2m as his fee. He lives on that during the life of the fund.
- If he's successful and the fund pays back the investors, he gets 20% of the surplus. The 20% is called *the carry*. If the fund turns into $400m, then $100m is paid back and there is $300m in profit. He gets 20%, which is $60m. This means the VC's real game is the carry.

The VC look bigger if you have a large office and lots of staff. He'll push you to hire people. He'll of course recommend that you hire his frat buddies, girlfriends, and slacker children.

If you understand the VC firm's business, you can deal with it better. If you're looking for $500K and your startup may sell for $100m, there's no point in talking with a $300m VC fund. They promised a 4X return to investors, which will be $1.2B, so they're hunting unicorns. If you exit for $100m, the VC gets $20m which will be only 2% of their $1.2B goal. $100m is big for you but it's small potatoes to the VC. Find a VC fund that matches your business model.

There are lots of details, but this is the general picture.

Wait, we have another question. Why is it called "the carry"? And why is it 20%? In 1,500 BC, the Phoenicians had a large Mediterranean merchant fleet which hauled olives, wheat, wine, lumber, and other things between Turkey and Spain. When you sent 10 tons of olives from Greece to Spain, they charged 20% to carry it, so they got 20% of the carry, which means their share was two tons of olives. Silicon Valley venture capital is based a 3,500 year-old business model.

Phoenicians only had to worry about sea monsters. VCs worry about investor clawback. If carry is paid out in year five but there's a loss in year six, investors use clawback to recover money. Yes, the VC has to return the money he made last year. If clawback is shared by the VC partners, they have to cover the loser VC. It can get pretty bad; sometimes, a VC must sell his house to pay the clawback.

Ask the VCs

Don't just answer questions. Ask questions.

- Are you investing in similar companies? If yes, they're funding your competitors. Whatever they learn from you, they'll pass it along.
- How do you choose your investments?
- Show us your list of investments for the last 10 years. Get the list and talk with them.
- What were the investment results?
- What boards are you on?
- What do you do day by day for your startups? Do you offer advice, referrals, customers, staffers, and contractors? Can you give examples?
- Why are you a good investor for our company?

The investment contract will give the VC a great deal of power over you, so be sure you understand how he works. Don't pay attention to promises. Call all of his past investments and see what they say. Look for startups that he didn't put on the list. Call them too.

Y-Combinator changed the VC game. Before YC, the VCs were the only source of money so they had power. But YC offered services, so now VCs have to actually do something for their startups.

Some investors will ask for seat on your company's board to keep an eye on their pretty money or because he or she really thinks they can help you run your business. Make sure he'll add value. Money is good but someone who helps with strategy is better.

➜ A founder has a list of questions at t2m.io/1BsCJCTn

Smart Money and Dumb Money

Another Silicon Valley idea is smart money and dumb money:

- Smart money is an investor who brings experience and connections. She can introduce you to co-founders, advisors, clients, and additional investors.
- Dumb money is an investor with no experience in your industry, has no connections, and doesn't understand investing. Kickstarter funding is dumb money because all you get is cash.

It's better to get smart money than dumb money, but there's an upside to dumb money: they won't bother you.

➜ A founder said this goes the other way too. Some startups only care about the money. They don't want to learn from the investor. The good investors have connections and experience and you should learn from them. Ask for advice and suggestions.

➜ Several of the founders met every two months with their investors. They updated the investors on progress and discussed changes in strategy. Other founders told me they only got money from their investors and no strategy. The investors left them alone.

Get Married with Your Investors

As you can see by now, investors aren't just money. When you get funding, you enter into a long relationship with your investors.

Just as you shouldn't get married on the second date, you shouldn't get funding quickly. Make sure that you and your investors are aligned with the project. If your goal is long-term development and investor's goal with short-term quick revenues, there will be problems.

Your investors may be on your board of directors, which gives them a great deal of power. If you disagree with them, they can block your decisions to force you to accept their decisions.

You need to be strategic with your investors. It's not just money. What else can they do for you? How can they help you? Good investors can introduce you to other investors.

➜ It's like getting married. Your ideal partner (whether your marriage or investor) will be a long-term partnership where you both work together to make it work. A good investor helps you to get deeply into an industry. She also has the financial connections and resources to keep you afloat in an economic downturn.

➜ It's not just the immediate investment. The investors will do the following rounds. If they cut off rounds, you're in trouble.

Problems with VCs

From experience, I'm cynical about VCs. Most engineers who've done startups have a negative opinion of VCs. But when I talk with VCs, they're really negative about VCs. Various VCs told me the following stuff:

- If the VC really thinks the startup will work, they'd sell their house, cash out their kids' college savings, take loans, and go all in. Which is what founders do. But VCs? Those manly champions of capitalism? No, they hide under the bed. They put in 1%, but only because they're forced by tax law.

- Why don't VCs just invest in startups that will be successful? Because VCs don't really know what works. They think they can make good guesses, but they have a 95% failure rate.

- Some VCs are driven by FOMO (Fear of Missing Out). They must get big returns or investors won't give them the money for the next fund. As a founder said to me, "no more limos and hookers!"

- Since VCs don't know what's going to work out, they spread their risks by sharing deals with each other. This creates a tight network that blocks outsiders. There are roughly 1,000 VCs in Silicon Valley who matter. Go ahead and guess how many are white guys from Stanford, Harvard, and Wharton.

- VCs start meetings by asking you, "Who else have you talked with?" No matter what you say, as soon as you leave, he calls the others to find out what they're thinking. Your NDA is worthless. So never answer this question. He won't answer many of your questions, so you don't need to answer all of his questions.

- VCs put a "right of first refusal" in your contract which means you have to ask them first when you raise more money. That sounds nice, but it means they can set the valuation. If another VC offers a higher valuation, the first VC can block him.

- VCs talk big about risks but it's not their money and they get 2% anyway. You do 80-hour weeks for two years, have no life, and live on cold pizza and warm Coke while the VC plays golf in the Bahamas.

- Some VCs see startups as a way to give jobs to their frat buddies and their loser nephews. I worked at a startup where the VC came in, demoted the CEO who'd built the company, and replaced him with his son who'd never had a job. Even the receptionist got more respect.

- There are VCs like to play psycho games with you. If they realize that you're desperate for money, they'll drag it out for weeks. What? You need to pay three months back rent this Friday or you and your dog get evicted? Let's meet next month. Or just a quick signature here and we get another 10%. We're just trying to help you, buddy.

Talk with Silicon Valley engineers who've dealt with VCs. They'll tell you more stories.

➜ The bad feelings happen because founders and investors have different goals. The VC's goal is to maximize value, which is VC talk for "make more money". They are not there to help founders. Founders in contrast work on their startups. When the VCs cut the money, the founders feel betrayed.

➜ Founders and finance people deal with the world in different ways. Founders, who are generally engineers, see information as something to share. If you're building a bridge, you share engineering data with the other engineers so it doesn't fall down. But finance people see information as something that should not be shared. The bank doesn't tell you that little ol' 4.6% interest rate will cost you $900,000 over the life of your house payments. It's in the engineers' interests to share information, but it's in the financier's interest to withhold information.

VCs in the World of Money

VCs have a big presence in Silicon Valley because people think a billion dollars is a lot of money. But Wall Street, London, Paris, and Zurich play a bigger game.

The US VC industry handles about $30B per year. Private equity (PE) works with $300B.

The really big boys are hedge funds which handle $2.9T. Nearly three trillion dollars. For them, the VC world is a rounding error.

Bridgewater, a hedge fund, alone handles $160B. That's 5X larger than the all US VC firms. Bernie Madoff's Ponzi fraud scheme was $50B.

Remember this when you talk with VCs; they're not in the big leagues.

Term Sheets

If the investors are interested, they give you a term sheet. This is a short (ten page or so) contract to state how much money, how much equity, and various conditions. It's written in legal terms, so you'll need a lawyer and a funding advisor to fully understand the implications.

For example, the term sheet includes lock-in, which means you must stop discussions with other investors and wait. You're locked in for four to six weeks until both sides accept or reject the term sheet.

However, the VCs aren't locked in. They can withdraw their term sheet any time, based on something they uncover in due diligence or they lost the money in Las Vegas. They won't tell you why they withdrew. They can lock you into a deal while they continue to look for better deals. The longer they wait, the more desperate you become.

Another game is the exploding term sheet. They offer it with a 48-hour clock. It has bad conditions but you don't have time to negotiate or understand it and you must accept quickly.

Dilution of Stock

Investors give money so the startup can grow. In exchange, the company issues new stock for these investors so they get a percentage of the company. However, this dilutes the percentage for the founders.

Let's use an example. You have a bottle of apple juice. You add a cup of water. You have more in the bottle but the juice is weaker. The same applies to funding.

- Let's say you and your co-founders have 80%. If there are three co-founders, each has 26.7% (a third of 80%) of the company. (The remaining 20% is the options pool for future staff and so on.)

- You estimate you need $200K for the runway. You offer 20% of the company to an investor if he invests $200K.

- The company creates an additional 200,000 shares for the investor. The investor pays $200,000 for the shares (one dollar per share). This brings your startup's valuation to $1m (if 20% is $200K, then 100% is $1m).

- The company now has 1,200,000 shares. The new investor has 16.66% of the company (200,000 divided by 1,200,000 shares = 0.1666 X 100 = 16.66%). He paid for 20% and gets 16.7%. A kind of magic, no?

- Your 26.7% co-founder share is also affected by the new shares. After the new stock is issued, your percentage drops from 26.7% to 22.3% (26.7 / 1,200 = 22.3%). You got diluted. You own less of the startup. On the other hand, the value of your stock goes up from $0.0001 to $1.00. Your stock now has value. Before, you had 26.7% of nothing. Now you have 22.3% of a million dollars.

Dilution is bad for early investors so they defend themselves with pro-rata rights (that's in the next section).

Each investment round dilutes the original team again. When founders are diluted down to 5%, they see there isn't much reason to work hard, especially when investors will get all the money, so they quit. Investors in some countries still haven't learned this. This is another reason that you shouldn't give your co-founders 5%. After a few dilutions, they'll quit. Investors learned it was in their own interests to not take too much of the company.

This is another reason to not have eight co-founders. Divide the 80% stock by eight and each gets 10%. With just a few funding rounds, they're diluted too far.

Pro-rata Rights

Another investor demand is pro-rata rights. If you raise additional money, he wants the right to buy more shares so he can keep his percentage of the company.

If the investor has 16.7% and you do another round of funding, his percentage will be diluted to 11.9% (16.7 / 1,400 = 11.9%). To prevent dilution, he can put in more money to stay at 16.7%.

However, founders don't get pro-rata rights so they're diluted with each funding round.

Preferred Stock

Another problem with investors is preferred stock. You have common stock, but the investor gets preferred stock. This means he has first rights to the money when you sell the company.

If he puts in one million dollars with a 10X return, he gets his $1m investment plus $10m of the sale. The remaining money is divided per stock ownership. If he has 30%, then he gets 30% of the remainder.

If you sell the company for $100m, he gets $1m, $10m, and then $30m. The remainder is for your team.

But that's the problem. The investor has little incentive to go for a big sale because he does well with a small sale, and it's easier to do a small sale. If he gets an offer for $10m, he sells the company and gets a 10X return. You get the remainder, which is zero.

Investors can also push the founders out, and if the founders haven't paid for their stock, they can seize the unvested stock. I worked at a startup where the VCs tried to fire a co-founder to get his stock, but the other co-founders threatened to quit.

When VCs fund a startup, the startup's incorporation is shut down and the startup restarts with a new incorporation. The VCs do this to make sure they're in control. A Silicon Valley billionaire used this to strip away stock from the founders. They had worked hard for years to build the company. He made more billions. They got nothing.

Are you starting to see a trend here? It's unfair, but they have the money so you must put up with them until you have your own money and don't have to deal with them anymore.

Your Long-term Funding Strategy

Up to now, we've covered the tactics and methods of funding. There's also the strategy to funding. Startup funding isn't just one round of funding after another. If investors get too much equity at the beginning, it becomes a problem because several rounds of dilution reduce founders to nearly zero.

You also need to consider the exit strategy. Some startups raise lots of funding and sell for hundreds of millions of dollars, whereas other startups raise only what they need and sell for less, yet the founders end up with more.

If your project works out, which means your project made money or at least didn't lose money, your investors hope you'll offer them to be part of your next project.

Work with your funding advisors, lawyers, and the investors who want a long-term relation.

What Are Current Trends in Funding?

This is a common question. By now, you know the answer. Trends don't matter. When you find a problem that needs a solution, you can build a startup.

The same with bubbles. Is there a bubble? Yes, of course. A bunch of unicorns are wildly over-valued. When the bubble pops, those of companies will vanish and the workers will be wiped out. But companies that solve real problems will survive.

Learn More about Funding

You're in a bad position against VCs. This may be your third or fourth startup, but the VC has done over 100 deals and spends all day playing golf with other VCs where they share tips on how to take more from founders.

Newspapers and magazines (including the *Wall Street Journal*) don't cover startups and venture capital very well. Journalists aren't finance people and don't understand what is really happening.

Here are a few places where you can learn more:

- VentureBeat.com: Website for the venture industry.
- Investopedia.com: Learn about investing.
- TheTrustedInsight.com: Limited partners (LPs are the ones who invest in VCs) use Trusted Insight where 60,000 LPs in 98 countries share information about VCs. It's Yelp for LPs.

You need funding advisors on your side who can negotiate with the VC on his level.

What about the Mid-stage and Late-Stage Phase?

If this book covers the early stage, what happens in later stages?

In the seed stage, your goal is to prove there is a viable business, which means you show it is profitable. If yes, it'll be easy to raise money.

That brings you to the mid-stage, where your goal is to expand your business, which means, increase your company's ability to make money. You are not developing the product anymore. Use investor money to hire lawyers, accountants, and CPAs to manage your company; you incorporate; you delegate the work of marketing, sales, and growth to people with proven track records. They come in as CMO, CSO, and so on. They bring along their network of managers, staffers, and contractors. At the end of mid-stage, you have a young company with all of its elements: production, marketing, sales, and financial operations.

In the late-stage phase, you maximize your company's performance to reach your potential market, compete against other companies, and position your company for sale (take-over), IPO, or long-term operation. Since this is a question about operations and management, it may be best for founders to step aside and let operations staffers manage the company. The founders can start the next startup.

This book is for founders. Founders start companies. Their best skill is in discovering and solving new problems that no one has seen before. Founders are at their best in the chaos of the early-stage startup. Staffers aren't good at that. Staffers are good at repeatedly performing processes.

When hiring your senior team, you're not hiring the person; you're hiring her network. For example, a good head of marketing has a wide network of marketing people where one is good at SEO, another at paid search, and others are good at social marketing, email marketing, print marketing, graphics designers, writing content, or analytics. They are willing to leave their current jobs and come to work for her. When you interview the head of marketing, you ask for these names and then contact her network. Did they work well with her? Was she a good leader? Will they join her in the new company? You give her a budget and leave it to her to bring them aboard. This means you hire an experienced team. They don't learn on the job: when they join, they immediately start working.

Summary: A Koala in a Barber Shop

After spending most of your time in the last six months on talking with investors, you finally get funded. You sign a pile of paper, the VC's secretary gets a table at Evvia, everyone toasts to the future, the VC give you a check, and at 11:45 pm, you go back to work. You can go to the next chapter.

How about a joke instead?

This founder meets with New York VCs. They say, "So what's your pitch?" and he says, "We're going to put a koala in a barber shop." The New York VCs say that's a ridiculous idea and they won't fund it.

He meets with Boston VCs. "What's the pitch?" "We're going to put a koala in a barber shop." The VC says, "Stop right there! Hey, guys, come and listen to this! It's the stupidest thing you'll ever hear!"

The founder doesn't give up. He comes to Silicon Valley and meets with VCs.

"So what's the pitch?"

"We're going to put a koala in a barber shop."

The Silicon Valley VC thinks about it for a bit and then says, "Wouldn't it be better with two koalas?" *

---

* Some reviewers said, "I don't get it". It's an SV joke. NYC investors don't take risks, so they say no. Boston VCs think they're smart so they insult founders. Silicon Valley VCs ignore reality and go for crazy ideas. Of course it's silly to put two koala in barber shops. It should be a kangaroo.

8: Boring Stuff: Finances

For a seed startup, you won't really have much in the way of finances. You're not making money and you don't have funding so there's not much to deal with. Don't hire an accountant or CPA yet.

There will be some costs. Keep track of them so you can be reimbursed later. These are your loans to the startup.

Collect everything: office supplies, postage, restaurant bills, bus tickets, train tickets, mileage, whatever.

On the receipt, write a short note to remind you what it is or who you met. When you drive to a meeting, write a short note, such as "Palo Alto to San Francisco, Dec. 7th, 2016, Twitter pitch event." Use Google Maps to find the distance and multiply by two for the round trip.

Get a large envelope or folder and throw your paper receipts in there. You can also use your cell phone to take photos of receipts. Save these until you get an accountant.

When you get funding, you'll incorporate and you can then hire an accountant or CPA who has experience with startups. She can advise you on the financial structure for your startup and organize your receipts and taxes.

Your accountant will figure out if a receipt is a valid business expense or not. If in doubt, throw it in there and amuse your accountant.

To find an accountant, talk with your advisors or friends who have built startups.

Money Stuff

As an officer of the company, you have a fiduciary duty to your investors. This legal term means you must manage their money responsibly. If you don't, your investors can sue you.

Don't use their money to party or buy yourself a Ferrari. If your investors find out that you're wasting their money, they'll shut you down. No more zoom-zoom. Keep receipts for every expense.

Open a Business Bank Account

When you incorporate, you get an Employer Identification Number (EIN) which you use to open the business bank account. It doesn't matter if you're a US citizen or not. This can all be done by email.

Using Your Company's Bank Account

Only the founder and perhaps one other should have permission to sign on the bank account.

Don't allow anyone else to sign the bank account. The bookkeeper or CPA may have view-only rights, but can't sign.

Several times, I've been at companies where trusted persons got into personal financial trouble and borrowed from the company bank account. They intended to pay it back but they couldn't.

This includes senior officers of the corporation. The CFO of a large Silicon Valley company stole $65m to cover his Las Vegas gambling losses.

Payroll

First of all, you shouldn't have any staff. That's for later. But there's lots of talk about payroll for startups so here's a few lines. And besides, this chapter will be too thin :-)

Believe me, it's a lot of work to do payroll. We used to do this at our startups. You don't have time for that. Use a payroll service. It's easier and cheaper than doing it yourself or hiring your own payroll person.

Your company has to withhold payroll taxes and pay those to state and federal tax departments.

In January, you send out W2 tax forms to your employees to show them their income for the past year so they can prepare their taxes. These have to be sent within a deadline. If you're late, there are penalties.

You also pay workers' compensation insurance.

You must also check your employees are authorized to work in the US.

If you hire contractors, you use an IRS 1099 tax form. You give the blank form to your contractor, who fills it out and signs it. You must get the signed 1099 form from the contractor before you pay him. A number of contractors know that if you pay first, then they won't sign the form and the IRS will force you to pay the taxes. Once you've paid, it'll be very hard to get them to sign the form. Since they want to be paid, you can ask them to sign first.

Y-Combinator's online information tells people that working for free is against the law and since you're an employee of your company, you must pay yourself a wage. This is incorrect. As a founder, you aren't an employee so you can work for free for yourself. You can choose to become an employee of your company and then you pay yourself a salary, but that's an option. If you hire staff in California, you have to pay minimum wage.

Yes, you can work for free. You have the right to exploit yourself. If you don't like it, you can form a union and go on strike against yourself. However, the strike can go on forever if management refuses to talk with the workers, so to end the strike, you start talking with yourself and everyone will think you're crazy.

Summary

A seed-stage should practically no finances. You should not be raising money, paying salaries, or making sales.

Just put your expense receipts in an envelope and when you get funding, hire an accountant to repay your team.

9: Selling Your Startup

For this chapter, we need a few more Silicon Valley terms:

- The Exit: The exit is your goal for the company. There are several ways to exit: you sell, you do an IPO, you shut down the company. People ask you, "What's your exit strategy?" or, "What's your exit?"

- Asset Classes: When you have $100m, your financial advisor will recommend that you diversify your wealth in four types of assets: cash, stocks, bonds, and alternative assets (such as land, buildings, artwork, diamonds, and so on). The ability to convert value from one asset class to another is liquidity.

- Liquidity: Let's say you have a one-carat diamond that's worth $1,000. The diamond and cash have the same value, but transactions with diamonds take time and you may not get the full value, so it has low liquidity (it's illiquid). The value of cash is easy to convert into other things (buy a cup of coffee, etc.) and you don't lose a percentage of the value, so cash is highly liquid.

- The Liquidity Event: That's when you sell your company. The liquidity event is the sale, merger, IPO, and so on. When you sell the diamond, you convert the value from diamond into cash. The same with your startup. Let's say its valuation is $10m. When you sell the company, you convert its value into cash.

- Acquisition: A company acquires your company, which means they buy your company.

- IPO (Initial Public Offering): When investors invest in your company, you're selling your stock to them. That's a private sale. Both sides know each other. You can also sell your stock in a market where anyone can buy as much or as little as they want and you'll likely never meet the buyers. That's a public stock market, such as Wall Street. The IPO is the first day that you offer your stock on the open market.

Liquidity and the Exit

The goal of business is a liquidity event, where you convert the asset (your company) into cash so you can buy other things (a house, whatever).

The business goal for your startup is the exit. There five possible outcomes, so let's first look at those and then talk about what they mean.

Five Ways Your Startup Will End

Key Idea: There are five ways your company will end:

- **Shutdown:** You set up the company, run it for a while, run out of money, and you shut down. It can be a graceful shutdown where you pay your bills, have a goodbye party, and return any leftover money to investors. Or it can crash into the ground, bills don't get paid, you run away from the mess, and staff smash the windows to climb in and steal their computers and office chairs (you think I'm making this up?). 80% of companies shut down within three years.

- **Zombie:** You start the company, but after a few years, it's only making $30,000 per year, which isn't enough to grow, but you refuse to give up because you can feel the Big Day is coming and this goes on for ten years until you finally crash. The company is a zombie because it's not dead or alive.

- **Lifestyle:** You set up the company, it's successful, and you're making $10-20m every year so you live the Good Life: big house, wife takes your two kids to play in the park, four cars parked in front, a boat parked in the Bahamas, a girlfriend parked in Las Vegas, and every day at two p.m., you go out to play golf. You and your VPs live like this for the rest of your lives. The company pays for your lifestyle. When you start your company, don't tell investors that you plan to do this. They want companies to grow big and have a liquidity event within four or five years. They definitely don't want to pay for your girlfriends in Las Vegas. Lifestyle companies are generally taken over by the kids who inherit. A few decades later, the grandchildren take over and usually sell the family company within a few years so they can invest in Big Things. A few years later, they've lost everything.

- **IPO:** You set up the company. Your team decides to go for an IPO. This will take five to seven years. Back in 2002, after the massive dotcom stock fraud, the US Congress passed Sarbanes-Oxley laws to protect investors. SarBox (or SOX) requires extensive financial and accounting tracking, so you'll have to raise another $5-10m to pay for SarBox compliance. Investment bankers work with you to prepare your company for the IPO. On the big day, you go to Wall Street and ring the bell. An IPO takes a long time and is expensive, so few companies go for IPO anymore. If the IPO doesn't work out, the company is sold or it crashes.

- **Acquisition:** You build the startup in order to sell it to a larger company. Your company is a take-over target. It has a small co-founder team, a few advisors, and perhaps a few investors. The company is sold within 12-18 months (or sometimes, in just a few months) for $5-10m. The buyer either buys the startup and you leave; they buy the startup and you stay; or they buy the startup, throw away the startup, and you stay. In the last example, this is an acquisition-hire (acquihire) where their goal is to get a strong developer team.

Of the five models, acquisition is the easiest to achieve. You work hard for a short time and then you sell the startup.

Your Strategy and Exits

The interviews with founders generally had a lot of comments about the exit strategy. The ones who'd done this several times said you may have a two- or three-year plan with an exit but as you develop your product and evolve from an early-stage startup to a mid-stage company, things will change. Your reasons and personal goals for building the startup will also change.

➔ During the project, focus on growing the company. The better the product, the more clients, and the greater revenue, the more value you'll have for the exit. What you'll sell is a company that makes money. Everything else is decoration on the cake. What they buy is the cake, not the candles.

➔ You should set a general long-term goal, perhaps $10m in 24 months, but have clear short-term goals. Every six months, step back and review your goals and how you see the project.

➔ Several founders told me that they started with the idea of selling the company, but after several years where you've put so much into it, it's hard to sell the company. It's like selling your baby.

➔ A nine-month exit is very fast. Some told me of three-month exits. It's generally twelve to eighteen months and sometimes three years.

Lifestyle companies are attractive because you set it up and live from it for the rest of your life. A hundred years ago, this was okay because companies could last fifty or seventy years. But today's global competition and rapid evolution of technology means that companies can do the same thing for only ten to twenty years. Companies must constantly innovate or become obsolete.

Exits and Your Investors

Discuss the exit with your co-founders and investors to see what they want. Develop a general plan with a timetable for goals.

Some co-founders want a quick acquisition where they work hard for a year, sell the company, make money, live on the beach forever, or move on to the next project. Other co-founders may want to be in a stable company for a long time.

The same with investors. Some want to invest their money and get a quick sale for a 10X increase in their investment. Others however want you to continue to grow the company for four, six, or ten years which makes more money for them. They want their investment to turn into a billion-dollar company. These investors see you as their employee. This is the reason for four-year vesting; the investors want to chain you to the company. However, there's no obligation for investors to stay.

There should be consensus among co-founders and investors on the exit. If some think it can grow into a billion-dollar company or they want a lifestyle company, they'll resist efforts to sell the company. If there's a $10m offer for your startup, you'll want it, but the VC wants a Dassault Falcon ($60m with onboard hot tub), he'll turn down the offer and ask for $100m. If it fails, he doesn't really care because he's rich already.

Nevertheless, co-founders and investors are interested in hearing about takeovers of other companies because it gives them an idea of the value of your company. Tell them if you know a similar company raised $2m and was sold to another company two years later for $10m with a 5X return.

➜ Somewhere in the beginning, you should think about what you want. Several people told me that when they started, they wanted money but after several years (and several startups), they realized they wanted their own company with a steady income. Others were happy to sell so they could start the next project.

→ The exit also depends on your market. Most markets are stable for years, but some markets exist only for a short period of time. Apps and games are markets where success is often measured in months. You can have a big hit but you can't expect another hit, so you should be ready to exit when the company is hot.

If You're Building for Acquisition

If you're building a takeover target, don't hire staff who won't be needed, such as sales and marketing, payment, accounting, and HR.

The buyer already has these teams and tools, so they'll just throw away these people and departments.

Don't sign long-term agreements for office space, office equipment, or company cars.

Why They Buy Your Company

There are all sorts of reasons for large companies to buy small companies:

- Innovation: Companies want to add new products. Cisco has bought over 130 companies.

- Future value: Your startup may only make $1m per year today, but it has the potential to make $10m per year in two years. The buyer isn't buying this year's value. The buyer wants the potential value in two years.

- Show growth: Large companies want to show growth to investors. This raises expectations of future growth, which raises the stock price. That's why Facebook bought WhatsApp.

- Enter new markets. Companies can enter a new market by buying an established company in that market. Google got into the mobile phone market by buying Motorola.

- Competition: Companies buy startups as part of their competitive strategy against other companies. Google bought Google Docs to annoy Microsoft Office.

- Acquihire: Companies buy startups to hire the experts. Facebook buys a six-pack of AI companies.

- Keep-away: Like kids in a playground, companies buy something just so another company can't get it. Oracle bought SUN to keep it away from Microsoft.
- Shut down potential threats: Companies buy potential competitors to get rid of them. Oracle bought PeopleSoft and shut it down.
- Stupidity: There are plenty of examples of deals that make no sense, such as AOL's $165B purchase of Time-Warner, which was a huge loss.

You can terrify the market leader with how fast you're getting customers, revenue, and market share. They'll buy you to add your numbers to their numbers, get rid of you as a competitor, or keep another company from buying you. You can also go to the number-two company and they'll buy you so they can become number one.

Which means you should be in contact with potential buyers at the beginning. Large companies have a VP of acquisitions who's in charge of buying companies. Find him, meet him, and stay in touch with him.

Valuation Models: The Price for Your Startup

Key Idea: You use valuation models to figure out the price for your startup. These models include:

- Cost-to-build plus a multiple
- Earnings plus a multiple
- Revenue plus a multiple
- Comparable deals
- Weighted average

Just as there are thirteen ways to look at a blackbird, there are many ways to calculate valuation. Let's go through these.

Cost-to-Build and a Multiple

How much would it cost the buyer to build the same thing? Add up the cost of a team, space, tools, investment, pizza, and so on. You multiply that by three years. Let's say it takes $5m to build the company.

$5m X 3 years = $15 valuation

It may take your team a year to do this, but that's dog years. Normal people need three years.

Earnings and a Multiple

You compare your industry's revenues against the industry's valuation. Find the revenues of every company in your industry. For example, five companies have $100m in total revenues (A = $10m, B = $20m, C = $30m, D = $20m, E= $20m). You find the valuation for the industry is $500m. The ratio of revenues to valuation is 5X, so each company's valuation is 5X of its revenues.

If your company's revenues are $10m, then…

$10m in revenues X 5X ratio = $50m valuation

Average Valuation

You find the valuation for the whole industry and divide by the number of companies in the industry to get the average valuation. For example, the industry's valuation is $200m and there are ten companies in the industry, so that's an $20m average valuation for each.

$200m total industry valuation / 10 companies = $20m average valuation

Comparable Deals

You find recent similar deals for buying other companies. In the last 12 months, four companies sold for $10m, $12m, $15m, and $8m for a total of $33m. Divide $33m by four companies to get $11.25m average deal.

($10m + $12m + $15m + $8m) / 4 four companies = $11.25m average deal

The Average of All Models

And then there's the average of all of the above. It may sound a bit dumb, but that's also a formula. You calculate each formula, come up with four numbers, and then find the average.

$15m + $50m + $20m + $11.25m = $96.25m / 4 = $24m average

Value per User by Valuation

Many social media companies use the value of each user based on valuation of the company. If a similar company has 100m users and it's worth $1B, then each user is $10.

$1B valuation / 100m users = $10 average value per user

You could also look at revenue per user (say, $20 per year) and then multiply by several years for a projected lifetime value.

100m users X $20 per user X 3 years = $6B valuation

Future Value of the Revenue Stream

You can also use the future revenue stream of the startup for negotiation. Instead of selling the startup for this year's revenues, you can show the growth record to show that the startup will have higher revenues in two years. You can use the future revenue to calculate the valuation.

Which Valuation Model?

There are yet more valuation models. Some founders built elaborate spreadsheets to calculate the valuation. Ask your co-founders, advisors, investors, other founders, and your M&A/IBs. They'll have more valuation models.

So which one do you use? All of them. Go through each formula and calculate the values. When you enter negotiations, you'll have more cards in your poker deck.

For more about deals, investors, and so on, see CapitalIQ.com and Pitchbook.com.

Buyer vs. Seller

It's also a question of what each side wants. If the valuation models say the startup is worth $10m but you want $30m, then go for that. Or the buyer will pay $7m but not more than that. How much do you want to get? How much is the buyer willing to pay?

The final number comes down to emotions and persuasion. An experienced seller can nudge the buyer to pay more. Or if you're desperate, you'll take less.

➜ If you estimate that you should get $20m, then ask for $40m. Or $100m. It's poker and there are no rules. The price is how much the buyer is willing to pay or the seller is willing to accept.

What about Unicorn Valuations?

A handful of companies have billion-dollar valuations. Uber's valuation is $70B, which is 7X greater than the value of the annual US taxi market. Snapchat loses $10m per month, yet it's valued at $25B. How does that work? That's the magic of capitalism! :-D

Twenty years ago, private equity companies waited for the IPO to buy the stock. Now, they're investing in pre-IPO unicorns and competing for stock with VCs. These investors will offer a higher valuation to be allowed to invest.

This is also an issue of supply and demand. Large investors who manage tens of billions of dollars need multi-billion-dollar exits but there are only a few unicorns, so they'll invest heavily in these companies.

➜ Some unicorns have become so big that they can change the definition of their market. For example, Uber started out as on-demand taxi, but they expanded the concept of their market by creating new kinds of customers, such as ride share, which didn't exist before. It's also inventing new markets, such as automated cargo trucks and automated delivery vans. When you click Uber in Dubai, Nairobi, or NYC, you can choose car or helicopter. If you consider the potential, it's possible Uber is undervalued.

There's another way to look at this. At some startups, the business model is to constantly raise money based on wild promises of $25B IPOs. At some point, that falls apart, but until then, there are seven fat years of big bonuses and great parties.

Wait, I see a hand in the audience. Yes, you in back. Okay, his question is, "How can a company be worth billions if it doesn't make any money?" That's a great question and you win a copy of this book.

Some of these companies are floating on big promises that investors should look to that far away horizon where the rabbits are singing, the deer are dancing, and the sun shines all night, and when we get there, everyone will be so rich that they'll be tired of being rich. For your small $10m investment, you too can be part of that adventure!

The VCs, the board, and others are making promises that may or may not happen, but today, they're taking money out of the company.

This is what happened at Theranos. A bunch of VCs and a board of super stars pumped it up to a $6B valuation on a product that never worked.

Today, the company is worth zero. On the bright side, Hollywood is making the movie with Jennifer Lawrence.

BTW, these companies are called "unicorns" because unicorns are fairly rare. There are +30,000 startups, but only a few hundred have billion-dollar valuations.

Silly Valuations

There are also silly ways to set the valuation. A startup met with a VC and asked for $7m. The VC asked, "Why seven million dollars?"

The founder said, "There are seven of us and we're worth a million each."

So the VC replied, "Why don't you grab two more people off the street and ask for $9m?"

Valuation and the Liquidity Discount

Remember at the beginning of this chapter that we talked about selling diamonds? You're going to find out one day that your $1,000 diamond will get maybe $500 when you convert it from diamond value to cash value. That's the liquidity discount.

If you want cash for your company, the buyer will push for a liquidity discount, which means he wants to pay less.

The liquidity discount can be 25-30% of the amount, so for a $10m deal, you'll get around $7m in cash.

This is one of the items in negotiation, so practice your poker face.

➔ A founder said there's no playbook for finance. Anything goes. Negotiations can be deeply irrational and emotional, filled with bluffs, threats, lies, and fake promises. This can be difficult for founders who are accustomed to dealing with engineers and computer science people.

Getting the Real Numbers

In the last few sections, I wrote that you should look up the revenues and valuations of companies. But that's difficult. Okay, it's impossible. Companies report their numbers only if they're obligated by the government and stock market. Otherwise, they don't tell real numbers.

A company may say it has $100m in revenues, but after it has been bought by a publicly-traded company that must file financial statements, its tax report shows it only had $5m in revenues. A private company's revenues are private information and they don't have to tell the public what they really made.

This means a private company's public number is part of their marketing. They talk big numbers. Yes, companies lie about their numbers.

When you try to find these numbers, talk with M&As, IBs, and investors; sometimes they know the real numbers or have a pretty good guess.

Your Numbers

What will you say on Facebook about your sale? Do you tell people that you sold your company for $20m? If you do that, everyone you've ever known will show up and ask you for money.

➡ It's best to not talk about the amount. You gain nothing by sharing the information. You can point to the non-disclosure agreement and say it can't be discussed.

What You Get

What can you get in an exit?

- Cash: You get $10m in cash.
- Stock: You get $10m in the other company's stock.
- Job: You get a job in the large company. You're now a desk monkey. Which will happen next? They fire you or you quit?
- All of the above: You get cash, stock, and a job.
- None of the above: The large company pays $10m, your investors take all of it (because they have preferred stock) and you get a T-shirt.

I hate to say this, but the last one is common. Many companies have successful exits (they made money) but investors take everything and the founders got several years of hard work and a deep hatred of VCs. A VC told me that happens in perhaps 30-40% of IPOs.

Cash, Earn-out, Distribution, Stock?

So what do you get? As you may suspect, this is another complex issue:

- You get a check.
- You get stock.
- You get an earn-out deal. This means you stay for a year (for example) and if you increase sales from $X to $Y, you get $Z. You have the big company's logo and sales team to get more sales.
- Or you get a distribution deal, which means you get X% of future sales.

Earn-out and distribution deals aren't good for you. When the large company takes over, their sales & marketing team is in control of your product. Sales people have spent years to build relationships with their top customers who buy known products. Your new product threatens their existing products, so they won't push your product. The buyer's upper management also realizes that they own your company and there's no reason for them to give you more money. Your product won't be a priority for anyone.

Just take the money and walk. You can decide what to do next.

That's why there's a liquidity discount. The buyer knows you want cash and you'll be willing to give up a bit to get that.

What about The Big One? Go IPO?

When you incorporate your company, your company is private in that you and your co-founders own the stock.

You can also offer your stock to the public. When your company is publicly traded, anyone can go to a stock broker to buy or sell stock in your company. IPO stands for "initial public offering," which means the first time you sell your stock in a public stock market, such as Wall Street.

Movies, TV, and books glorify 21-year old founders who IPO and make $5B in one day.

It happens… but behind that story, there's a different story. The investment bank that handles the IPO will pay to place news stories in newspapers, magazines, and TV to create a frenzy among investors. The investment bank sets the price to $30 per share, sells huge blocks of stock at $20 to their frat buddies at large banks, and when it IPOs and there's lots of news, the little people rush into buy stock and the price goes up to

$75 so the big banks sell their $20 shares the same day and make a fortune. A few weeks later, the stock drops to $40. Vast amounts of money were transferred from little investors to the large investors.

It gets worse. The investment bank knew the stock would go to $40, so they underpriced it at $30. Their insider friends make money but your company gets ripped off because you should have gotten $40 but most of the stock was sold for $20. You lose hundreds of millions of dollars. It's an insider's game.

As CEO of a public company, you have to keep the press and stockholders happy. If the quarter's numbers go down, clueless financial journalists attack you, your stock drops, and you're on an endless numbers treadmill.

That assumes you'll still be the CEO. When VCs go for IPOs, they're dealing with other finance people and all of them prefer to work with CEOs with MBAs and M&A experience. Generally, you'll be replaced as CEO. It's a skill to build a new company; it's a different skill to deal with investment banks and Wall Street who have been doing this for years.

A note about public markets. Just as there are public markets such as Wall Street for selling publicly-traded stock, there are private exchanges such as SharesPost.com and NASDAQ Private Market where you can sell non-public stock. But if co-founders start selling their pre-IPO stock, it can affect the valuation. Talk with your financial advisors about this.

What's the Best Model?

You put together a small team. You bring in a few investors who understand what you're doing, support you, and agree with your overall plan, including your exit strategy. You work hard for a year or two and sell the company.

When you start your second startup, your top team and investors will come along, plus your business contacts, vendors, suppliers, and so on. Everything goes faster because you'll avoid mistakes. You'll have close relationships with customers and they'll tell you what they really need.

Summary

So this VC dies and goes to heaven. But when he gets to the Pearly Gates, St. Peter tells him that Heaven's quota for VCs is all filled up. No room for another VC.

He thinks about it for a while and then steps up to the gates and yells, "Hell is about to IPO!"

The gates burst open and hundreds of VCs come running out and head down.

St. Peter says, "Well, we have an opening, so you can go in."

And the VC says, "I think I'll follow the boys, I can't miss out."

10: The Acquisition

Along with updating the book, I added this new chapter on acquisitions to the book because people kept asking me for more details on how to sell a startup.

How to Build a Studio in Palo Alto

But first, a short story. I have a small house in Palo Alto. We have a big backyard so a few years ago, we decided to add an extra room to our house where my mom could live. We planned it as a studio with its own small kitchen, bathroom with shower, sliding glass doors, and so on.

I talked with a few building contractors but they wanted quite a bit of money (it's Palo Alto) so I began to look into building it myself. Although small Palo Alto houses are worth more than large East Coast mansions, they're just small simple houses, built with basic lumber and stucco walls. I bought several books and, yes, I could build this.

However, Palo Alto's building code has a very high standard. How high? Palo Alto uses the ISO standard for the Building Code Effectiveness Grading Schedule (BCEGS). There are about 20,000 cities in the US and Palo Alto's building code puts it in the top ten. The building code book is the size of a telephone book, and I don't mean the telephone book for Buck Snort, Tennessee (that's a real town) (next to Mousetail, Tennessee).

If we were in many other cities, we could build it ourselves. But Palo Alto rules are so detailed that only building contractors with experience in working with Palo Alto's building inspectors can do the work. How detailed? One of the carpenters put in the foundation nails sixteen inches apart. No, the code required fourteen inches. Take them out and do it over again. Construction took six months (anywhere else, it'd be done in a month), the inspectors came every two weeks, and many things had to be re-done.

Although the building code requirements added time and work (and costs), the studio turned out very good.

What's the point of this story? This chapter is about selling your startup. The basics of selling and buying are simple. But not when selling a startup in Silicon Valley. Just like I couldn't build the studio by myself, you can't sell a startup by yourself. A Palo Alto startup can be anywhere from $20 million to several hundred million dollars and some have sold for billions of dollars. These deals involve founders, investors, lawyers, brokers, and companies, all of whom have complex legal rights and obligations, which means a mistake can either be very expensive or worse, kill your startup.

For example, a company (you know their name) signed an NDA, copied a bit of code, ha! ha!, and a few years later, before it could IPO, it had to pay about a billion dollars to settle that NDA.

In this chapter, I'm not going to tell you the specifics of how to do a sale. That's not possible because, just as I can't summarize Palo Alto's 533-page building code plus the hands-on knowledge of Palo Alto building contractors, carpenters, plumbers, and building inspectors in twenty pages, nobody can summarize how to sell a Silicon Valley startup.

What I can do is give you the overall picture of what it's like to do Silicon Valley deals so you'll have an idea of what to expect.

For this chapter, I interviewed founders who've sold their companies and lawyers and investment bankers who've handled dozens of startup acquisitions.

The Dark Secret of Deals

Although the sale of a startup is one of the main goals of business in Silicon Valley, there's very little information on how to do this.

I also found people don't talk about deals. When a company buys another company for the revenue potential and competitive advantage, the information is extremely valuable to their long-term business strategy so why should they tell their competitors?

There's also another reason: many deals turned out bad, so why talk about that and look bad?

The business press (Wall Street Journal, Fortune, and so on) rarely describe how a deal was done. Business articles are written by business journalists, who weren't part of the deal or don't really understand business, so they didn't really know how it happened.

A rare example of an insider's description of a deal is *High Stakes* by Charles Ferguson, who built a Silicon Valley company and played Microsoft and Netscape against each other to sell his company. Because he made enough money that he never had to deal with Silicon Valley again, he talked about many well-known Silicon Valley people (read a summary at t2m.io/PKupeOC8). This is another aspect of business: there's not much advantage in publicly attacking a jerk because one day, you may have to do business with him. People either praise him or say nothing, which makes it difficult for outsiders to find out about people.

Just as there isn't a standard method or strategy to build a startup, there isn't a clear process to sell a startup. There are many haphazard ways to do a deal. In the rush to get it done, many of the parts of a deal are often confused or just never cleared up and that's left to whomever takes over after the deal is done. Negotiations often happen between people who aren't lawyers and can't really read legal contracts. As you'll see later in this chapter, many founders don't really understand what corporations are nor their own lawyer's role in the corporation. They may have lawyers, but they'll ignore the lawyers. There is also strong pressure of time, because if it's done too quickly, there can be a bad deal and if it takes too long, the deal can die. In one case, the buyer asked for an extension to tomorrow morning and in the morning, he backed out of the deal. Many people are involved in the sale, each has his own understanding of the deal and each has his own goals. There can be problems within your own team: some want the deal at any price, others want more money, and some don't understand at all. The same may be true for the other side. Several people said to me that doing a deal is like trying to herd cats.

➜ Startups are like making Hollywood movies: it's a combination of passion, dreams, technical complexity, organizational skills, big promises, a lot of bluster, people with oversized egos, and maybe a bit of artistic talent. Talk with people who work in Hollywood and they'll tell the crazy stories of how movies got made. We assume Hollywood and Silicon Valley are different because one has actors and the other has engineers, but the deals are generally made the way.

It's widely written that only one out of 400 startups get funded and only one of twenty startups have a successful exit, but that assumes they all have an equal chance, which isn't true. The majority of startups are weak ideas or don't have good teams so they never really had a chance. There are also many great startups, but they don't show their value to potential buyers so the startups are never acquired.

A startup may be in an accelerator or incubator, but sometimes, it doesn't mean much. Some of these places are daycare centers for startups. The staff are tracking meaningless statistics, such as number of pitches, percentage of occupancy, and so on. Often, to fill seats, they'll accept startups that don't have a chance. Sometimes, to "show diversity", they'll accept certain startups. If you're considering an accelerator or incubator, ask how many of the startups were successfully sold.

→ In interviews, people told me that in several decades of experience, 95% of people are honest, but 5% are swindlers. They don't have the education or skills and they know it, so they'll do whatever they can to make (okay, steal) money. This is just like in football which has rules and teammates on your side, but a football player has to look in 360 degrees: one of his teammates could slow down and let an opponent tackle him. Most of your team are on your side, but some may not be.

A good team is like a good relationship where everyone does more than required. You want long-term relationships, camaraderie, chemistry, and collaboration. You don't have to cover your back. You should enjoy working with them. Be sure they know there are penalties such as exclusion or blacklist. Be sure to highlight the future benefits.

Although you like your partners, you still have to be sure about them. There are Silicon Valley CEOs with fake engineering degrees and VCs with fake MBAs diplomas from Harvard or Stanford which were bought online. As I wrote earlier about due diligence, if the business has value, you need to carry out due diligence on everyone in the deal, including your co-partners, your lawyers, and your brokers. Trust is good; verify is better.

→ Several interviews told me that deal-making in Silicon Valley is like a marriage, but they also added that the business relationships are often more important than marriage, because a marriage can end in divorce and the two never speak again, but in Silicon Valley, deals can fall apart but if everyone made an honest effort, people will work together for the next deal.

If the founder is a 21-year old who has only held summer jobs, he has no idea how to do a $100m deal, no matter how many TV shows he has watched. You may hear that a 21-year did a $500m deal, but in reality, a team managed the deal. The investors put a young person as a figurehead for the press while they do the deal in the background. Several major Silicon Valley companies were started this way.

This network of connections and skills also means that deals flow upwards. The little guys can do little deals, but when a large deal come along, the little guys know they don't have the connections to get it done so they pass it to large dealmakers who can get the deal done and the little guys get a referral fee.

There is lots of money, but few viable startups. The few good startups have the advantage because there is too much money but only a few good startups. Founders think that they need investors, but in reality, investors need the founders. There are tens of thousands of investor millionaires but there only a few hundred good startups each year in Silicon Valley.

These are some of the reasons for the tightly-closed social networks in Silicon Valley. I've learned it's the same way in real estate, diamonds, medicine, fine art, and many other industries. There is always a wide circle of people in each industry, but the hardcore, which is about ten percent, are the experts who really know the ones who are good (or aren't), have the top skills, and know what's going on. They're the key connections within the industry.

➜ When you start building your startup, write a strategic investor roadmap with the goal of an exit. Find out who you should talk with and build connections to reach those people. As you build your startup, ask your advisors, mentors, and lawyers if the startup if the startup is sellable. There are lots of startups with active teams and good ideas, but they'll never be bought because there aren't the right kind of buyers for them. It's good to start discussing this early in the process. Ask if they know of similar deals. They may know potential buyers and you can start talking with them to see if there is interest.

The Players on Your Side

Let's start with the players on your side of the table. This includes your co-founders, staff, your advisors, your lawyers, and your brokers.

The Founders in an Acquisition

Your first startup is like your first house: you'll waste money on needless improvements, expensive carpenters, and lose money on a bad mortgage deal that was recommended to you by that nice banker on TV. If you pay attention, you'll do better the next time.

This is your first startup. Everything is new to you. But the advisors, investors, investment bankers, and buyers have done this many times and they know much more than you.

It's important that you show that you can learn from mistakes and listen to your advisors. Advisors, investors, and lawyers have worked with dozens of startups and they notice very quickly if the founder is not coachable. When they see he won't listen, they walk away.

➔ For example, a startup in its seed stage had not yet gotten any investor money, so the team was taking side projects. The CTO however refused to take side jobs in programing and insisted on being an Uber driver. Not only it paid less, it showed a lack of common sense. He wouldn't listen. The investors walked away.

➔ Another common problem happens when the CEO founder sees the startup as his baby. He won't accept advice or ideas from others that may change his idea. Investors have also seen that and they walk away.

➔ Investor also want to know if a co-founder has the personality to attract, hire, train, manage, and lead people. A startup was looking for funding and the CTO said, "I don't like to work with people." The investors walked away.

As a founder, you should ask your advisors, lawyers, and brokers what to do, what to expect, what to avoid, and how to plan and build the path to liquidity. You don't have experience in this; they do, so ask them to guide you. They want to ensure a good outcome, so they'll help you.

How to Build Connections

I hope by now that you see that connections are an important part of your startup.

Just as there is dumb money and smart money, there are also dumb founders and smart founders. A dumb founder just builds a product. Without a strategy or connections, the quality of the product won't matter because he won't be able to sell it.

A smart founder builds a long-term strategy. She builds this exit to make the money and connections to set up a startup for the second exit, which builds the money and connections for the third exit and so on. Each success will be larger than the previous one.

You should contact alumni office of each of your co-founders. Send a letter (with your pitch deck) and highlight that the co-founder is an alumnus. University alumni associations want to brag to their alumni, current students, and potential students that an alumnus is building a startup. The best networks include Stanford, Berkeley, MIT, and Harvard because they have produced many angels, VCs, and brokers.

Your advisors, mentors, and lawyers can make introductions to investors and potential buyers. The heads of accelerators and incubators also have extensive networks and can make introductions.

Your business bank can also make introductions to their banking clients. For example, Silicon Valley Bank has many major corporations as clients so they're like a social network hub for Silicon Valley.

Look for other relevant startups that got funding and ask them for introductions. VCs invest in similar startups to spread the risk so they talk with other VCs to share resources, information, and connections.

You can also use your city's Chamber of Commerce to make connections. If you want to meet with, for example, Husqvarna, you can quickly find their US headquarters are in Charlotte, North Carolina. You join your city's chamber of commerce and meet its corporate relations person and ask for an introduction to the corporate relations person at Charlotte's Chamber of Commerce. That person will set up a meeting.

Your city may also promote you to other cities, even if they don't really like you. If there's a possibility to bring business to your city, a city mayor may do the introduction. The mayor can also often fix local laws for you. San Francisco tells companies they should move to San Francisco because Twitter and Uber are based in San Francisco, although they have bad relationships with those two.

There's another way to meet companies. In the lobby of incubators and accelerators, the logos of their corporate sponsors are shown on what is called the trophy wall. These are the companies that are interested in startups from the accelerator or incubator. Go to the lobby and take a photo of your co-founder and make sure the trophy wall is in the background. The accelerator has a bizdev person who maintains connections to the corporate sponsors.

If there is a company that you want to meet, ask the accelerator's bizdev guy to introduce you. You don't need to be in the accelerator program: the bizdev guy gets points for introducing you. Give him your pitch deck and he'll introduce you and pass your deck along. You can also do this on the web. Accelerators and incubators have a web page where they show off their successful exits.

Finally, use a spreadsheet to keep track of connections. There isn't a software to manage business connections (and that'd be a good idea for a startup). People use Excel, Word, and similar.

➜ The best way to get connections is to do good work. Build a great seed stage team and product. People will see what you're doing and they'll tell others.

Your Lawyer's Role

Founders tell me they have a lawyer, but no, they don't really have a lawyer. Most founders don't understand the lawyer's role until it's too late.

Let's look at the concept of a legal person. If you're 21 years old in the US, you're a legal person which you have the right to vote, sign contracts, and so on. You can lose these rights in certain cases (coma, mental disease, criminal sanctions, etc.)

Under US corporate law, a corporation is a fictional legal person. The law treats the company as if it was a person. Guided by its human board, it can also enter into contracts. Both a real person and the fictional corporate person have a range of rights and the corporation's lawyer represents and protects those rights.

This means when you as a founder hire a lawyer for your startup's corporation and the lawyer is hired and paid by your corporation, the lawyer represents the interests of the corporation, not your interests. It's his obligation as a lawyer to represent and protect the company's interests. If he doesn't protect the corporation, he can be put before the Ethics Board and he can lose his law license.

That's the legal theory. Here's the reality.

First-time SV founders see only the current project and don't think about the long term, building a long career, or building relationships. The lawyer however thinks about his 30-year career in Silicon Valley. The big investors are here for decades. If the lawyer wants to be invited to future deals (and future legal fees), he protects the investors' interests because the money is in the long-term relationship. Your startup's lawyer will tell you this if you ask him directly.

➜ For example, a small car parts maker invents a new device for cars but large Detroit car makers copy it so the small company hires Detroit lawyers to sue. Detroit's top lawyers and automotive industry executives grew up in the same neighborhoods, went to the same private schools and same universities, belong to the same fraternities, are members of the same country clubs, and their children go to the same private schools. His new Detroit lawyers will advise him to settle. They won't piss in the pool.

➡ If you want to sue (for example) Google, you must hire a lawyer who is far away from Silicon Valley, such as Arkansas, and doesn't care about his future in Silicon Valley.

Because the lawyer represents the startup corporation, not the founders, it creates a conflict-of-interest between the startup's lawyer and the founders. This means your startup's lawyer may often advise decisions that are not in your interest. If you hire your own personal lawyer, she may advise you as a founder to make decisions in your best interests (which are not necessarily in the interests of the startup or the investors). The conflict of interest can come out during the acquisition negotiation, so often, each founder may have to hire his own lawyer to represent him against the other founders and the startup (which is represented by its own lawyer). Meetings become interesting when everyone at the table has his own lawyer.

Dealing with Investors during a Sale

Investors have one question, "What's the chance that I'll get my money back and what's the multiple?" Okay, that's two questions. Many investors are doing several investments at the same time, so they're not really into the details of your project.

➡ One interviewee told me the key issue for many investors is liquidity. While there's lots of talk about building a better world, social equality, blah, blah, blah, many investors care only about money. Talk with your investors and find out what they really want.

➡ Another said nearly the same thing, "Investors really want only to know how much money they'll make and how fast they'll get their investment back again. That's the key factor in more than 99.9% of their deals."

➡ Some of the investors will be hands-on, while others are hands-off. Let the hands-off investors know that the hands-on investors understand what is going on, and they'll leave you alone. For example, a startup was doing ERP software (enterprise resource planning) and the investors didn't really understand the ERP business, but Cisco and other large companies were interested in buying the startup and the lead investors understood the market, so the investors went along.

➡ Another problem with dumb money is the extra trouble. You get the investor's money, which is good, but the investor bugs you with questions and advice for the rest of the marriage. Smart money knows when to leave you alone. A startup was holding a weekly investor presentation but the lead investor found it took five hours to prepare and deliver, so he changed it to once a month so the founders could concentrate on meaningful work.

➔ Several said to me that getting involved with investors is like a long-term marriage with children. If the relationship is good, the investors will work with you through several startup projects. But if the investors are difficult, it can make life miserable.

➔ It's dumbfounding how seed-stage founders have an almost universal belief that investment money is free money. It's as if they think if the startup crashes, no big deal, they'll just go on to their next startup. If you waste time and money, that'll follow you around for years.

➔ Accept second-tier and third-tier investors to get first-tier investors. When you show that you can get investors, the first-tier investors will become interested. This is like dating 4s and 5s to get a 9 or 10.

➔ When investors see a fire, they'll pour gasoline on it. So you must show them the fire. If you can show growth in key metrics (users, revenue, and so on), they'll give you money to increase that growth.

➔ In the hills of Palo Alto, deer run with other deer and mountain lions hunt with other mountain lions. What happens when a deer wanders into the lion's territory? They get eaten. Investors invest seven days a week, twenty-four hours a day. Startup founders enter the investors' world only occasionally. I think founders should find advisors and lawyers whom they trust and let them lead in negotiations. When they get back to their offices, the lawyers can explain what happened and what to do next.

The M&A Investment Banker's Role

The connection between your startup and the buyer is generally an investment banker. There are sell-side and buy-side investment bankers: one represents the sellers and the other represents the buyers. Although they're called investment bankers, they're not bankers. A better description is financial engineers who work with money.

An investment banker is also called an IB, i-banker, ibanker, or an M&A broker (mergers and acquisitions). In this chapter, I'll use broker as the general term and talk only about sell-side brokers.

Good brokers are their late 30s to early 60s. They live in Silicon Valley, which means from San Francisco to Saratoga, and mostly clustered around Palo Alto, and they're active in pitch events, investor events, conferences, and so on. They're always looking to see what is going on.

Brokers are small (they handle deals in $30-to-100m range), mid-size (in the $500m range), or large (they handle deals that are $1B or more.) Brokers are not interested in $5m deals because these are too small. Get your sales up to $10m to get their attention.

Generally, your lawyer can introduce you to a broker. Another way is to attend large conferences. The keynote speakers often know the acquisitions team in their corporations. If you know family funds or advisors to family funds, talk with them because they also often know M&A people.

You hire a broker with a $100K start fee and an exclusivity agreement, which means you can't work with another broker. The broker's fee can be 2% to 5% plus $5-10K per month. Or he uses the Lehman Formula, which is 5% of the first million; 4% of the second million; 3% of the third million; 2% of the fourth million; 1% of the fifth and following millions; or 5-10% of the total sale. All of this is negotiable.

It may sound high to pay a 5% fee to the broker but that's good for you: the more the broker earns, the higher the final sale price.

A broker with ten years of experience has done perhaps 50 deals. This means they have substantial experience in acquisition. This also means that both sides (sellers and buyers) have established traditions and a mutual understanding of the process, often from both sides of the table. Every deal is substantial amount of money, so they don't want to waste time if amateurs try to tell them what to do.

You should talk with at least three M&A brokers and choose one.

The broker must have an SEC license and obey SEC rules for deals. If someone offers to do the deal for you for a small fee, it's possible he doesn't have a license. If the sale is done, you can refuse to pay his broker fee. The buyer can also refuse to complete the deal and make a substantially lower offer. The SEC also offers bounties to catch brokers without license.

What the Brokers Do

The broker prepares your company to be sold, researches the market, writes reports on the market, identifies potential buyers, meets with them, finds the best offer, and closes the deal.

The brokers use their own research teams and they also buy research reports.

They also have a worldwide personal network of senior executives in their target industries to get an insider's view of the market.

The broker's business analyst team researches the market for your startup. For example, if you're building software for the automotive industry, they look into that market.

They find perhaps 100 potential buyers. The buyers are sorted into A, B, and C groups. The A group is the ideal buyer. The B group is acceptable. The C group are buyers without any good reason to buy your company. If you see a company was bought by another company but nobody can explain the deal, it was probably a C-sale.

The broker's analyst team write reports that starts with an understanding of your startup's financials and potential. It looks at the state of the market: the players, companies, and customers. This includes how the market is structured, such as vendors, suppliers, sub-manufacturing, and distribution. They identify which companies are potential buyers (and which aren't) by looking at the company's position within a market and whether it is growing, stable, or declining.

They can estimate the impact to a company if it buys your company. This means how far would it place them ahead of their competitors in terms of revenues, transactions, markets, and so on. The projections can be anywhere from five years to twenty years.

The brokers use their personal networks to get personal introductions to the buyer team. They show the buyers why they should buy your company. This includes additional revenue, new products for their product line, access to new markets (either new categories or new territories), competitive advantage, and the impact on stock value.

This research is shown to potential buyers over a series of meetings to build interest and convince them to buy your startup. The brokers also pressure buyers on the need to move quickly and, if necessary, FOMO (fear of missing out).

She shines the apple. She'll talk with potential buyers to create auction fever. She'll tell each one, "We're talking with other buyers"; "You'd better hurry"; "Because you're my special friend, I'll let you get this!"

An M&A deal can take nine months in a series of steps for research, reports, due diligence, meetings, bidding, and the closing transaction.

The large buyers also have their own research analysts who do the same research from their side. On some issues, they may agree and on other issues, they disagree. The heads of the buyer team look at their research and compare with your broker's reports.

Analysts treat numbers with skepticism and try to find other sources for confirmation. Because there is so much money in a deal and not much transparency, there are opportunities for fraud. For examples of M&A fraud, see my notes from *Investment Banking: Valuation, Leveraged Buyouts and Mergers & Acquisitions* by Joshua Rosenbaum and Joshua Pearl (Wiley, 2013, 988 pages). Go to t2m.io/6tfi9ZxM

➔ Of course, this is what happens at sensible companies. As we've all seen, some companies go into deals that make no sense at all. This is often the result of a lack of direction from top management.

➔ Several founders said this depends on the country. Silicon Valley has been here for several decades so are lots of brokers with connections and experience. However, other countries don't have experience. Their brokers have little idea what to do. The startups work with their investors and advisors to arrange the sale. Due to US government regulation and Wall Street rules, there is transparency about financial data in Silicon Valley. But in many other markets, it's the wild west. Anyone can say anything and it doesn't matter because six months later, everything changes. Founders who learn quickly and move fast can grow in chaos.

➔ A bunch of years ago, two Stanford students came up with a software tool. I wrote the documentation and website. We built everything on Stanford's servers. The two engineers also brought in a woman as the M&A broker. We estimated it would take six months so we wrote a specs list (what the tool would do) for her and she began shopping it around. At the end of five months, she told six large companies that she and a lawyer would be in Room 88 of the Palo Alto Hilton at 4 p.m. on July 16 where the companies could deliver their bids. Two hours later, she congratulated the winner. The company announced next morning that it had developed the tool. The product had a working title that was a variable in the software: just change the title and the product had a new name. It was a successful product and many of you used it. The entire team was six people; everything was done from home; we only met in person a few times.

What about MBAs?

Can you hire your buddy the MBA to do this for you?

An MBA is Masters of Business Administration, which means they're trained to manage large companies. They're not trained to sell companies (or build and manage startups). Business schools don't teach any of this, just as law school doesn't teach you anything about the reality of being a lawyer or opening a law office.

Furthermore, if your MBA friend doesn't have an SEC broker license, the deal may fall apart.

What about Placement Agents?

A placement agent is someone who sells your company by adding your startup to a list of available companies, which is available online (for example, BizBuySell.com). People who want to buy companies can look at the list.

However, this makes a bad impression on investors and buyers. It's a sign of desperation. The pretty girl doesn't need to place ads. Companies that use placement agents are generally going out of business, the partners are fighting, or the founder is retiring. Any of these means it's a bad company.

How to Find Analyst Reports

You can get analyst reports on companies and markets if you have an account at Charles Schwab or any of the online brokerage services (Fidelity, E*Trade, and so on). There is also Yahoo Finance Report Screener at finance.yahoo.com/screener. Reuters also offers reports. The prices vary.

There are many independent analyst services, such as ChainBridgeResearch.com, IndependentGlobal.com

Deloitte's *M&A Making the Deal Work* is a useful overview in only 130 pages of the M&A process (see t2m.io/ZyOX9m2B). They also publish reports on the expected direction of M&A activity. See Deloitte's website (at t2m.io/iAMdiH0q) for more information.

Position Your Startup for Acquisition

You should learn as much as you can how your market works, from production to channel to distribution.

If you're lucky, you can find some of this research. If one of your co-founders is studying business, is an MBA, or you know someone who is in business school, you may be able to get access to a Bloomberg terminal at a business school's library. Some of your investors or investment bankers may also have Bloomberg terminals. Bloomberg terminals have thousands of analyst reports.

Documentation for Acquisition

Your startup's documentation is a collection of the code, legal contracts, and information. This shows the buyer what he is buying. It shows the full value of your business, which enhances your valuation.

Documentation includes the following:

- **Resume and short biography for each co-founder:** Your team's profiles should also show their ability to shepherd a company through the acquisition process
- **Pitch deck:** The pitch deck should include a video that demonstrates what your product does, how it works, and the value to the customer
- **The business plan:** An outline of your strategy to liquidity. This is also useful to show to investors so they can that you know what you're doing. They'll join and recommend you to other investors.
- **The software code:** Code, libraries, tools, languages, and so on.
- **Data:** Show how you got data for your software. The data should be clean, which means you show it was properly acquired and there are no legal problems.
- **The intellectual property (IP):** Show that you own the IP. If one of your co-founders is still in college, the school may have an IP clause that owns whatever she develops while she's a student. If one of your co-founders is working a day job at a company, the employment contract may state that the company owns any IP that he develops while he is an employee, even if he does this at home on weekends. If there are potential owners of your IP, talk with them to get a release. If your startup is valuable, the college or company will certainly look for their share.

- **Copyrights and trademarks:** Show who registered them, when, payments, and so on. These should be registered by the startup corporation. If you registered them yourself before you incorporated, then write a document that transfers your ownership to the corporation.
- **Contracts:** All legal agreements with co-founders, staff, contractors, consultants, advisors, and investors, including office lease agreements and so on
- **Financial:** Cap table, financing, accounting, and bookkeeping
- **Connections:** Your network of leads, clients, customers, advisors, investors, partners, attorneys, investors, M&A brokers, customers, buyers, and so on

The documentation should also discuss any potential legal problems or liens.

You should also document your process towards acquisition. This includes a list of contacts and meetings.

Always keep your startup's documentation up-to-date. A good way to do this is to keep the documentation in a cloud drive so everyone in the sell team has access. When you sell the company, you transfer the drive's login and password to the buyers.

➜ One startup was built with software licensed from other companies, which meant they didn't own anything, so they had nothing to sell. Even though it had revenue and was a successful as a business, it couldn't be sold.

➜ Another startup had $400K in revenues and 40 customers but the business was based entirely on handshake deals. There were no contracts. If they sold the startup, the customers would likely leave because they were not bound by contracts so there was no long-term revenue potential.

➜ If you have a lease for your office, it can be an asset or a liability. If the buyer can sub-lease or transfer the lease, they won't lose money (and may even make money if the lease is cheap in an expensive market).

The Negotiation

The Team on the Seller's Side

The seller team should be only two co-founders. This keeps it simple. If you have three or four co-founders, decide on two to handle the sale and the others should accept this.

Never go to a meeting alone. Always bring your partner. Always have two in the room on your side to be sure that you negotiate well. One talks while the other listens and takes notes. Afterwards, review together what was said. Also take note of face expressions and body language.

You're at a great disadvantage. Everyone else in the room has five to ten years (or more) of experience in acquisition. They also have a deep personal network of experienced people for advice and information. You have practically none of this.

On your side, you have your attorneys, perhaps some of your lead investors, and your broker. Talk with them and discuss the options.

Handling the Negotiation

The more buyers in competition to get your startup, the higher the price and better terms that you can get. You want multiple potential buyers to keep your dating options open. Don't get too in bed with one buyer.

If a buyer realizes there are no other buyers, he'll take advantage of this to offer a lower price.

Don't disclose the names of potential buyers (the persons or companies) to anyone unnecessarily. Silicon Valley is deeply interconnected and everyone knows everyone.

When you begin negotiating with a potential buyer, there may be an agreement on the negotiations.

there may be an agreement to negotiate in good faith. Neither side wants to waste time. These agreements are legally enforceable.

The terms may include negotiation in good faith, a right of first notice, and a ban on shopping around.

If the potential buyer has a right of first notice and you find another buyer who makes a firm offer, you must notify the first buyer who then has the right to accept that offer. He generally has a time limit (for example, sixty days) and if he doesn't exercise his option within the time limit, you can sell to the second buyer. If you sell without notifying the first buyer, you'll see lawyers dancing around your office. Both the first and the second company will sue you.

Another clause includes a five percent breakup fee if the deal fails. If you spend three months and then the buyer backs out, he has to pay five percent of the purchase amount. This protects your time. However, if there are onerous clauses, you can abandon the deal.

There is also "certainty of closure". The founder should make best efforts to close the deal. This includes participating in all meetings, delivering documents, and so on. It also includes convincing co-founders and staff to stay after the purchase. You can offer bonus or rewards if they stay for another year or two.

There may also be a ban on shopping around. You won't be allowed to talk to other potential buyers to find a better deal or better options. This creates complications. Some people sign the agreement but continue to talk with others. In whatever market you're in, the list of potential buyers is small and they generally know each other, so it's possible your buyer may find out that you're secretly dating others. The buyer will see whether your moral values are honest or devious. If the buyer finds out but wants to do the deal, he'll go ahead but he'll remain suspicious of you. If you stay in the startup as part of a takeover, you may not be able to move up the ladder at the new company.

Your M&A broker will walk you through the agreements and explain the implications.

Preferred Stock and Veto Rights

Part of selling your company is to be sure that you're actually able to sell your company. You may have 51% of the company (or 75%) of the company, but that doesn't mean that you can sell the company.

Your investor has preferred stock which means it gives the investor a veto right over any sale or transfer of the company. This protects the investor from a quick sale of the company at a low value.

This also creates a conflict of interest between the founder and the investors.

The veto basically gives the investor the power to force a higher sale. For example, a company wants to buy your company for $20 million. You may have 75% of the stock but a preferred investor with only 10% believes the company can be sold for $100 million, so he'll veto the sale and you'll be forced to work for two more years to get a higher valuation. It may be true that you'll get $100 million later, but it also means two more years of long hours at a low founder salary while the investor floats around the Bahamas in his yacht with an all-girl crew. Or two years later, the market changes and you get nothing but the investor doesn't mind because it was just a small part of his investment portfolio.

Preferred stock also means the investor stands first in line for the money. Let's say the investors put in $1m and the agreement has a 10X multiple. If the startup sells for $10m, they get all the money and you get nothing. This means if the investors can sell the startup for $10 million and recover their investment and also make 10X, they likely will. There is little reason for them to wait another year on the possibility that it may go to $20 million so the founders can get some money because there's also a risk that the investors get nothing. This is a reason to not raise too much money. If you take too much funding, you'll lose much of the profit due to the preferred multiples. The more you raise, the less you get. Take only the funding that you need. Talk with your advisors and lawyers about this.

Another problem comes up if the buyer offers acqui-hire as part of the takeover. Instead of $20 million, the buyer offers $5 million and hires the founder team for $250,000 per year per person for four years plus $500,000 bonus if you stay all four years, plus company stock. That's great for you, but the investors get nothing from that so they'll definitely veto. Back to cold pizza for two more years.

If you accept the takeover offer, you'll have to stay at the new company for four years to get the final bonus. Four more years of cafeteria food. No Bahamas for you. That's golden handcuffs.

You may own 75% of your startup and every business school will say you have control, but you don't really have control.

➔ Several startup co-founders told me that they didn't know about this. They got an offer from a buyer but some of the investors vetoed the sale because they wanted more, so the founders worked for several more years, the market changed, and the startup became worthless.

➔ Other founders told me they built a company, sold it for millions of dollars, and got nothing. The investors got all of the money due to the preferred stock.

➔ Business schools don't teach any of this. Most business school professors have never built startups, raised money, or sold a company.

Managing the Buyer's Team

The buyers sit on the other side of the table. Here are several tips on how to handle the buyer team.

Just as you should not negotiate alone, the buyer won't be in the room alone. There will be a team to manage the flow of discussion, supply information, handle any objections, and most importantly, watch your words and body language for clues.

While this is the first time for you to sell a company, the leader of the buyer team has ten years or more experience. He started as an assistant and sat in on many negotiations before he did his first deal. He may be very friendly and personally charming, but that's part of his methods. There are lots of books and seminars on how to negotiate and he'll likely test several methods on you to find what works. This is why you shouldn't negotiate alone and why you need experienced experts on your side.

Every conversation is part of the negotiation. When the buyer suggests getting together for a casual lunch, play a round of golf at his club, or go for a hike in the hills above Palo Alto, it's all part of the process. Steve Jobs often did business deals by suggesting a long walk around the neighborhood. A number of CEOs take people on hikes to see how they behave.

When you research the buyer company, look at the history of the executives that you'll be meeting. If he's new, very often he's rising which means he's aggressive and will want a quick deal where he feels that he won. If the executive has been with the company for a long time, he may be conservative, which means he'll be cautious and slow in the negotiation. Consider this and see how you can use it. If he's aggressive and wants a quick win, start at a high number and then drop your number on condition of a quick sale to let him think he has won. If he's conservative, settle in for a long discussion and answer all of his questions. When he's satisfied, he'll buy.

The purchase isn't just about the technology. The buyer is also looking to see if there a cultural fit. Will your team work well together with their larger team? Does your team have the same general values and attitudes as their teams? This also includes questions about your commitment to staying with the startup as it becomes part of the larger company. Some founders may say they need a break or be eager to start the next project but that doesn't sound good to the buyer.

There's a problem in the relationship between seller and buyer. During the negotiation, the two sides are adversarial, but after acquisition, they should be collaborative. So be careful not to be too aggressive because it may create problems after the deal. Again, like dating, if you're too hard in the pre-nuptial agreement (such as bringing in a team of lawyers against your girlfriend), you can be sure there's going to be trouble in the marriage when she sets her lawyers to watch you.

Try to find out why a company wants to buy your company. They may actually want your company. But they may secretly buy you as part of their strategy to intimidate another company. They may not really care about you or your team, and when they get what they really wanted (the other company quits the market), they'll walk out of negotiations or, if they bought you, they'll just shut down your team. There have been famous examples of this in Silicon Valley.

Corporate buyers tend to be in their mid-40s to late 60s, which means they learned sales from traditional sales people, such as Zig Ziglar, who was a superstar in sales in the 70s and 80s. These salesmen developed methods with names such as the puppy close, the portrait close, the assumptive close, and many more. It might help you to buy one of Zig Ziglar's books, such as Ziglar on Selling (1991). I've worked with more than 300 clients and I learned a great deal of sales from these books. Whatever you're selling, the basics are the same.

But all in all, there isn't much room for maneuver. The buyer has done many deals and knows what is possible or not possible. By the time you get to the table, he has likely already done substantial due diligence and research on you, your team, and your startup so if you're there, he's confident he can conclude the deal easily and quickly so he can move on to the next deal. At one large Silicon Valley company, the VP of acquisitions is expected to do ten deals per year, which is about one per month. Listen to the experts on your team, because they want to get things done so they too can move on to the next deal.

What's the Valuation?

In chapter nine, I wrote about valuation models. The chapter showed you several valuation models so you can estimate the value of your startup.

But in reality, valuation is done by the broker's business analysts. They research the market to find the optimal range for your startup's value and then advise the broker and that's what he takes to the table.

There are things that you can do to increase your valuation. The first is to be sure that your side clearly knows your business value. This also means your co-founders, advisors, customers, lawyers, investors, the brokers, and so on should know your business value. Meet with each one privately and ask a few simple questions, "what do you think our startup does? What is the value that it offers to a buyer?" You'll find out many in your network (including some of your co-founders) aren't clear about your value, which means you didn't communicate it well to them, which means you're not communicating it to outsiders. Write a clear message about your startup, show it to each one, and ask them again until they get it.

→ If you show potential, buyers will want to meet you. If you're not getting meetings, you aren't showing potential. Either you have it but you don't show it, or you just don't have it. So again, make your business value clear on your website and to your team (co-founders, customers, advisors, lawyers, and so on).

→ I'm an advisor to a number of startups. I've found over and over the co-founders often didn't agree among themselves on what the startup did. Often, the staff and contractors had only a vague idea what the startup did.

In the early stage of your startup, start thinking about who could buy your company. Look at the five or ten top companies in your market space and understand their business. Look for the gaps in their business. Can you fill that gap? Make sure the buyer understands the gap and how you can fill it.

You can also often meet with the VPs of acquisitions at those companies while you're still in the seed stage or mid-stage. They'll tell you what they want to see in the startups they acquire. For example, they'll tell you the KPIs, such as monthly revenues, number of customers, transactions, market share, or the rate of growth in revenue, customers, and transactions. You can build towards those KPIs.

→ Don't sell. Don't make it look like you're desperate to sell the company. Show your value and let them think that you can be bought. Your startup should be the attractive girl at the dance. By appearing reluctant, you'll attract more buyers which lets you choose and you get a higher valuation.

Ask your advisors, angels, brokers, and so on to suggest a price for your startup. Because many of them have been involved in deals that were never made public, ask them for comparable deals. You should ask them independently in private meetings to avoid group-think.

But whatever valuation you have, never tell the buyer. Let the buyer state the price. Sometimes he'll state a number much higher than what you thought.

There is also the question of "material issues". The SEC defines a material issue as information where there is a substantial likelihood that a reasonable investor would have considered the information important in making his or her investment or voting decision. Read the SEC's statement at t2m.io/8VeZFR1X and discuss this with your lawyers. If you tell your buyer that the eggs are rotten, then it's okay to sell rotten eggs. But if you don't tell him, then the buyer can sue for his losses. You must disclose all problems to your buyer. Talk with your lawyers about this.

Who Makes the Decision?

In a corporation, the concept of chain of agency defines who can make decisions at the different levels within the corporation.

First, let's look at the decision-making process in the startup:

- The shareholders appoint the board of directors (BOD). The shareholders give the board the power to act as an agent for the shareholders.
- The board in turn appoints the CEO, CTO, CFO, and so on as officers of the company. These officers have power to make decisions on the day-to-day operations of the business.
- The officers appoint managers, who hire staff, contractors, and so on.
- Any change in direction of the business must be approved by the board of directors.
- But a sale of a substantial part of the assets of a business or the entire company (such as an M&A sale) must be approved by the shareholders. The board of directors or the CEO and other officers don't have the power to sell the company.
- In a sale, the shareholders can appoint an agent (for example, the broker) who has the power to represent the principal (the company) and bind the principal to a contract.

On the buyer's side, the decision to buy a startup depends generally on the size of the deal. Each company's corporate bylaws set the limits, perhaps as a percentage of the company's annual revenues, such as 10%, or a number such as $50m. At most large companies, the VP of acquisitions can buy companies up to a certain amount. Google's M&A team has a $100m annual budget to buy ten companies per year. At other companies, the officers (CEO, CFO, and so on) can approve M&A deals. And for some companies, the board of directors (BOD) makes the purchase decision. If the acquisition is so significant that it changes the core business of the company, it may need to be approved by shareholders.

When the negotiations start, the broker will check to see if the person on the other side has the authority to make the deal and how much he can spend without triggering additional approval.

In general, the larger the deal, the more complexity, so more approvals will be necessary. Deals over $80-100m bring in more review teams, decision-makers, lawyers, financial teams, SEC filings, and so on.

→ The size of your buyer is also a factor. The buyer generally wants to make a deal that moves the needle. For a billion-dollar corporation, a $10m deal won't make a difference. The founders may be approaching large companies but the deals are too small so nothing is going to happen. Either look for smaller buyers or increase the value of your company so it makes a difference to a large company.

→ Many small deals are never published. The deal wasn't particularly good for the seller. Several friends built a startup, raised ten million dollars, worked for five years, and sold the company for ten million. The investors recovered their money, but they lost money in the sense that they could have put their money in Wall Street and made 12% per year (so they would have made perhaps $6 million). The founders worked for five years and got nothing. The purchase agreement included an NDA so the founders just say they can't talk about it and everyone thinks they made money.

→ There's an advantage in buying a small early-stage startup. Small startups are nimble and in close contact to the current market. That's valuable information to a large company, which enhances the valuation. Perhaps that's what Facebook saw in Instagram. Mark Zuckerberg bought Instagram in 2012 for a billion dollars. At the time, Instagram had thirteen workers, zero revenue, and only 30 million users (some Youtube cats have more followers), but it was growing fast and their users spent hours on it. Mark turned out to be right: Insta has grown to a billion users. From 2015 to 2017, it made $13B and will produce $7B in 2018. Young users are switching from Facebook to Instagram, but that's okay because Facebook owns Instagram. In 2014, Mark Zuckerberg bought WhatsApp for $17B. Although he owns only 28% of the stock, each of his shares has ten votes, so he has 60% of the votes. This gives him total control of Facebook.

The Big Picture

The Silicon Valley Assembly Line

Many have written that the metaphor for Silicon Valley is a biological eco-system, like the rain forest of Brazil.

But a rain forest ecosystem isn't the right metaphor, because ecosystems don't include a social network. I don't mean Facebook. Animals and plants in a jungle don't collaborate. Eco-systems are systems of predators and prey. Some are food for others.

In contrast, Silicon Valley has a complex social network of people and teams that cooperate, where one cycle can take several years, and the participants collaborate throughout their thirty- or forty-year careers.

The business press, both magazines and TV, generally either don't describe it or don't realize this they because they're not part of it. This is largely invisible to outsiders. When people visit Silicon Valley for a few weeks, they see lots of meetings in coffee houses but they don't see the overall picture.

Okay, I'll admit, there's some truth to the ecosystem metaphor because some Silicon Valley CEOs and VCs act like sociopathic predators. They buy companies to destroy them or attack their competitors. But they're the exception.

Key Idea: The best metaphor for Silicon Valley is the assembly line in automotive manufacturing. At Ford, Honda, or any large car company, there's a assembly line about 1,200 yards long (about 1.2 km). The car moves down the assembly line and at each station, people or robots build the engine, paint the frame, install dashboards, seats, and doors. Smaller teams prepare parts for the assembly line teams. Smaller companies also build parts and deliver them just-in-time to be added at points along the assembly line. A car with about 30,000 parts is built in about 19 hours. Watch a video at t2m.io/V5HvKtR1

About the same happens in Silicon Valley:

- A founder has an idea for a startup and puts together a team of co-founders.
- A few people see the project's potential and they begin to help to build the startup. The circle of experts may include advisors, mentors, professors at Stanford and Berkeley, accelerators, and incubators. They have ten years or more of experience in Silicon Valley. They give advice, make introductions, and watch how the team performs.
- The circle around your seed startup will let begin to let others know further down the line, such as lawyers, angel investors, venture capital, large law firms, business banks, and M&A brokers. Like car assembly teams, each has skills and roles. They cooperate to pass it down the line to their trusted connections.
- A car may be built in 19 hours but it can take several years to build a startup. The lawyers prepare the founder agreements, the incorporation, the business contracts, and begin introductions to investors.
- The teams often know the other teams up and down the line and they talk, share information, and collaborate.
- Many investors know each other and when one finds a good opportunity, he tells the others.
- As the startup moves along, the lawyers and investors bring in investment bankers and brokers.
- The goal of the Silicon Valley assembly line is the exit (the liquidity event), where the startup is sold and turned into money or stock pay the co-founders, advisors, lawyers, investors, and M&A brokers.
- Each team does its part of the work, either paid, a share of the outcome (i.e., stock), or both. This means everyone in the process is invested in the outcome. There's little point for anyone to help a startup that will never have a chance because they won't make any money.

Another name for the Silicon Valley assembly line is *deal flow*. About 70,000 deals go through Silicon Valley every year. Because there's lots of money in this, people want access to the deal flow. Since it's impossible to know which startup will succeed, people try to part of as many deals as possible.

If the experts have the feeling that an early-stage startup will fail (such as signs of poor leadership, a weak team, a lack of IP, and so on), they won't pass it down the line because it will damage their credibility and relationships. The startup won't get help, connections, or investments and it eventually fades away. In effect, the startup is ejected from the assembly line without realizing this happened.

Because people further down the line are so busy and there's so much money involved, they don't want to waste time to deal with amateurs who won't listen.

Key Idea: This is the general entrepreneurial mindset of Silicon Valley: a large web of people who share knowledge, skills, and experience and collaborate on many projects over decades.

Conclusion

Remember what I wrote at the beginning of this chapter about building our studio in our backyard in Palo Alto? In most places, you can just get your cousin, his pickup truck, some lumber, and build it yourself in a few weekends.

And in many places, you can sell a small company by yourself and maybe your sister-in-law the lawyer can help.

But selling a Silicon Valley startup is a complex process so you'll need to work with advisors, mentors, lawyers and brokers who know what they're doing and who will guide you along the process.

However, whatever you're selling, both sides know what is being offered, how much will be paid, and when the deal will be done. Both sides understand the process and both sides want to get it done.

Further Reading

David Smith is both an engineer, a lawyer, a startup founder, and a patent broker. He has also done many deals. His books cover the legal and financial details of business in Silicon Valley.

- *Zero to IPO* by David Smith. Appendix 1, 2 and 4 covers valuation, negotiating the deal, and the M&A process. At Amazon. Free PDF at zero-to-ipo.com or tynax.com/z2ipo.php
- *Dollar Value* by David Smith. Covers valuation techniques and how they apply to startups. Published by Cambridge Manhattan Group. Free PDF at tynax.com/dollarvalue.php
- *Patents, Cloaks & Daggers: Inside the Secretive Patent Trade* by David Smith. Published by Cambridge Manhattan Group, LLC. This book explains the role of patents, strategies by corporate decision-makers,

and the patent wars with special emphasis on high-tech and the patent trading marketplace. Free PDF at svbs.co/images/Patents-Cloaks-and-Daggers.pdf

- An IP Strategy to Protect Your Business: A Primer on Developing and Implementing an Effective IP Strategy by Greg W. Benoit. Published by Tynax, 2017. Free PDF at tynax.com/ipstrategy.php
- Investment Banking: Valuation, Leveraged Buyouts and Mergers & Acquisitions by Joshua Rosenbaum and Joshua Pearl (Wiley, 2013, 988 pages)

11: Life after Your Startup

So what do you do after your startup is done?

If it was successful, you recover. Travel. Teach. Be an advisor or angel. Write books. Go and sit on a beach and mediate until you gain the deep spiritual awareness that it's boring to sit on a beach.

If your startup failed, get up, brush the dust off, and get back on the horse.

After you've done this a few times, be an advisor and help others to build startups. I'm an advisor to nine startups.

You should also teach. It's a lot of fun and you'll learn more than your students. I teach at a French business school in SF.

Become an angel investor. After a few startups, you'll have some money to invest in startups.

Where Fail Is a Good Word

Everywhere else in the world, failure is a bad word. You blow up a company and nobody will talk with you.

But in Silicon Valley, failure is okay.

Why? Because we know 95% of startups fail. We've all worked at failed companies. Peter Theil, who built three unicorns, also built 200 failures.

If you paid attention and learned from your failure, you'll do better next time. Because you got experience and connections, it'll be easier to build your next startup and get co-founders, advisors, and investors.

What the Founders Say

→ One founder told me that of course, she'll start on the next one, but for now, she can't imagine what that will be because she's so caught up in the current one.

→ Another founder said his startup could grow to become a billion-dollar company so he expected he would be in it for the next seven or ten years.

→ Several founders said their market was something that will always be around and it's a worldwide market, so they expect the company will last a long time. After it's well-established, they'll build more companies.

→ Other founders told me that they took long breaks between startups. Some travelled around the world for six months.

→ Some founders said the goal wasn't important; startuppy life is so much fun.

→ Another said she couldn't imagine doing anything else.

→ Many founders plan to give money to help others, especially in education and health. One person told me that he wanted to sell his startup for $400m. I asked, "Why 400?" He said he needed about $10-20m for his family to be financially secure. He'll use the rest of the money to buy a 100X100 mile block of forest in northern Canada and set up his own private national park where the animals can live free forever.

In Closing

If you're thinking of doing a startup, there are no clear paths up the mountain, many tigers, lots of monkeys, many places to fall off, and it's always night. Don't listen to the villagers' folk tales. Build a good team. Get a few good Sherpas. Push forward. There are many paths to the top.

And if it doesn't work, take a break and try again.

Your second and third startup will be easier. You've learned what works and avoid what doesn't work. You'll have many friends who've done it and they'll help. Founders share and help each other.

As you saw, the founders whom I interviewed were incredibly open and helpful. When you build your startup, talk with other founders. It's a great community.

I wrote this book to share experience and information with you so you can avoid a few mistakes and be more successful. Let me know what works or doesn't work.

I'm working on my next book. Want a free copy when it comes out? Subscribe to my newsletter at http://eepurl.com/wC-C1 or at my website.

Good luck!
andreas
andreas.com

Extra Stuff

Website for this Book

Lots of stuff at the webpage for this book at andreas.com/book-startup.html

- **1-page business plan**. Your business plan on one page.
- **10-page pitch deck**: A sample Powerpoint for your pitch deck.
- **Books to read**: Founders listed several useful books.
- **Books by me**: Books and eBooks on SEO, Google Ads, KPIs, ASO, Twitter, content marketing, and how to write books. Some are free eBooks and others are at Amazon.
- **Websites & blogs**: A bunch of blogs and sites that founders said were useful. The clickable list is at the webpage for this book.
- **Useful blog postings by me**: Details on how much you make with digital ads; how to test your grandmother pitch; virality (plus research papers), +225 ideas for growth hacking, and more stuff.
- **Associations**: List of Silicon Valley associations and groups.

You can get legal documents such as incorporation, term sheets, NDA (non-disclosure agreement), stock distribution, and capitalization tables for free at LegalZoom, Nolo, and Clerky.

You can get free business plans at BPlan.com.

Index

500Startups, 36
Accelerators, 35, 137
Acquisition, 120, 134
Advisors, 26
Alumni office, 139
Aqui-hire, 152
Assembly line, 158
Beach
  Finding, 11
  Gallop in the surf, 31
  Live forever, 123
  Spiritual awareness, 162
  Watch birds, 19
Berkeley, 38
Blank, Steve, 67
Board meeting, 78
Broker, 143, 144
Broughton, Ronda, 6
Business bank, 140
Business bank account, 118
Business plan, 60
Carry, 106
Cats
  Board of directors, 78
  Bury, 49
  Co-founders, 24
  Funny Videos, 65
  In Google, 47
  LinkedIn, 61
  Not lawyers, 74
  On conference calls, 30
  Pixs, 3

Chamber of Commerce, 140
Chang, Claire, 6
Chung, Patrick, 6
Chunn, Bob, 6
Co-founders, 23
Connections, 9, 15, 16, 108, 139
  How to build, 139
Contact me, 3
Convertible notes, 103
Co-working spaces, 35
Deer, 143
Desks and chairs, 44
Digital presence, 17, 41
Dilution, 111
Documentation, 148
Dogs
  Bark in conference calls, 30
  Bite silly people, 76
  Cemetery, 49
  Certified, 17
  Dog food, 72
  Dog years, 18, 125
  Dogfooding, 62
  Evicted, 110
  Facebook, 61
  Follow CEOs, 71
  Run away, 14
Due diligence, 103
Dumb money, 108
Eco-system, 158
EIN, 118

Elevator pitch, 61
Email newsletter
  Monthly, 50
  Scrub the list, 51
Employer ID Number (EIN), 118
Errors
  Did you find one?, 2
Estanislao, Edgar, 3
Exit, 120
Facebook, 157
Ferguson, Charles, 136
Fitzpatrick, Rob, 54
Flynn, Shawn, 6
Founders Space, 35
Funding, 87
Ghafourifar, Alston, 6
Ghafourifar, Mehdi, 6
Ghattas, Cyril, 3
Gil Amat, Gala, 3, 20
Gong, Zhihong, 2
Gong, Zhihong, 6
Google
  Adwords, 45, 47, 48
  Analytics, 45, 48
  Search Console, 48
  Suite, 44
Grandmother pitch, 61
Hedge funds, 111
Hoffman, Reid, 16
Hoffman, Steve, 6
Hollywood, 136
IgniteXL, 35
Incorporate, 76
Incubators, 35, 137
Initial Public Offering, 120
INSEEC SF, 3
Instagram, 157

Intellectual property, 85
Interview
  Questions to ask, 56
  Your customers, 53
Investment bankers, 143
Investors, 87, 94, 142
IPO, 120
Isper, Ed, 6
Jobs at startups, 14
Katzenjammer, Anaximander, 2
Key Ideas
  Assembly line, 158
  Connections, 9
  Entrepreneurial Mindset, 160
  Five exits, 121
  Grandmother pitch, 61
  Interviews, 53
  Pitch deck, 96
  Questions to ask, 56
  Valuation models, 125
Keyword research, 48
Kim, Dale Ho, 3
Koala bear, 116
Koltek, Tim, 6
Kopas, George, 6
KPIs, 66
Labat, Alain, 6
Lawyer, 74, 141
Lean startup, 67
Legal stuff, 74
Lehman Formula, 144
Lifestyle, 121
Link, 146, 147, 158
  andreas.com, 2, 20
  Business plans, 60
  BuySell.com, 147
  Data Validation, 51
  Deloitte, 147
  Newsletter, 3
  Tynax, 160

Yahoo Finance, 147
Links, 10, 35, 36, 42, 59, 63, 64, 108
Liquidity, 120
M&A, 143
Material issues, 156
Merger & acquisitions, 143
Metrics, 66
Microsoft Office, 44
Milliken, Eric, 6
Morris, Ron, 6
Mountain lions, 143
Namgostar, Ginger, 2
Negotiation, 150
Octopus, 30, 73
Palo Alto, 10
Parrish, George, 6
Petkanic, Donna, 6
Phoenician ships, 107
Pitch, 61
Pitch decks, 95
Preferred stock, 151
Private equity, 111
Private national park, 163
Ramsinghani, Mahendra, 6
Rickman, Eliza, 2
Ries, Eric, 67
Rodriguez, Adrian, 6
SEC, 156
Silicon Valley, 9
Simon, Barry, 6
Smart money, 108
Smith, David, 6, 160
Stages of a startup, 115
Stanford University, 38
Startup documents, 60
Studio in Palo Alto, 134
Term sheet, 111
Trigger, 84
Unicorns, 128
Valuation, 154
Valuation models, 125
Venture capital
  VC firm, 93
  VCs, 87
  Venture capital, 87
Vesting, 82
Veto right, 151
Viral marketing, 64
Visa, 31
Website, 43
Whiteboard, 44
Y-Combinator, 35
Zombie, 121

www.ingramcontent.com/pod-product-compliance
Lightning Source LLC
Chambersburg PA
CBHW071541220526
45469CB00003B/875